PRIVILEGE AND ANXIETY

PRIVILEGE AND ANXIETY

The Korean Middle Class in the Global Era

Hagen Koo

CORNELL UNIVERSITY PRESS   ITHACA AND LONDON

Copyright © 2022 by Cornell University

All rights reserved. Except for brief quotations in a review, this book, or parts thereof, must not be reproduced in any form without permission in writing from the publisher. For information, address Cornell University Press, Sage House, 512 East State Street, Ithaca, New York 14850. Visit our website at cornellpress.cornell.edu.

First published 2022 by Cornell University Press

Library of Congress Cataloging-in-Publication Data

Names: Koo, Hagen, 1941– author.
Title: Privilege and anxiety : The Korean middle class in the global era / Hagen Koo.
Description: Ithaca [New York] : Cornell University Press, 2022. | Includes bibliographical references and index.
Identifiers: LCCN 2022003849 (print) | LCCN 2022003850 (ebook) | ISBN 9781501764912 (hardcover) | ISBN 9781501764943 (paperback) | ISBN 9781501764936 (pdf) | ISBN 9781501764929 (epub)
Subjects: LCSH: Middle class—Korea—Economic conditions—20th century. | Middle class—Korea—Economic conditions—21st century. | Income distribution—Social aspects—Korea.
Classification: LCC HT690.K8 K66 2022 (print) | LCC HT690.K8 (ebook) | DDC 305.5/5095190904—dc23/eng/20220204
LC record available at https://lccn.loc.gov/2022003849
LC ebook record available at https://lccn.loc.gov/2022003850

Contents

Acknowledgments	vii
Note on Transliteration	ix
Introduction: The Fractured Middle	1
1. The Rise and Fall of the Korean Middle Class	19
2. Rising Inequality	34
3. Consumption and Class Distinction	53
4. Class Making, Gangnam Style	67
5. Educational Class Struggle	83
6. In Pursuit of Global Education	101
Conclusion	118
Notes	129
References	133
Index	143

Acknowledgments

During the years I was working on this book project, I accumulated numerous debts. First, I would like to thank the Center for Korean Studies (University of Hawai'i), the Asiatic Research Center (Korea University), and the Korea Foundation for providing financial support for my research. I also wish to express my gratitude to several institutions that provided a pleasant environment for my writing as a visiting scholar: the Australian National University, the Seoul National University, the Free University of Berlin, and Tübingen University. While working on the manuscript, I was given valuable opportunities to present my arguments in talks at l'École des Hautes Études en Sciences Sociales, Toronto University, York University, SUNY-Binghamton, the Seoul National University, the Free University of Berlin, Tübingen University, and the Korea National University of Education. I wish to thank the audiences of these talks for their many insightful questions and comments on my work. My former colleagues at the University of Hawai'i were always supportive of my research and were willing to read and give feedback on my drafts; I am particularly thankful to David Johnson, Le Lin, Young-a Park, Manfred Steger, Patricia Steinhoff, and Myungji Yang. Outside the University of Hawai'i, my special thanks go to H. H. Michael Hsiao, who triggered my interest in the middle class by involving me in a comparative research on East Asian middle classes, and to Kwang-Yeong Shin, a premier scholar of social inequality in Korea who generously shared his data with me. I would also like to express my special appreciation to several of my former students who helped me with data collection at various stages of my research, including Jaehoon Bae, Ki Tae Park, Haeeun Shin, and Seung W. Yang. Finally, I am grateful to Sarah Elizabeth Mary Grossman at Cornell University Press for handling my manuscript with care and efficiency.

But most of all, I would like to express my deepest appreciation to my partner, Jean Young Kim, and my daughters, Jennifer and Christine, for their love and support. Jean Young shared the joys and frustrations of writing with me during the long years I have been working on this project. I dedicate this book to her.

Special Acknowledgment

This work was supported by the Core University Program for Korean Studies through the Ministry of Education of the Republic of Korea and the Korean Studies Promotion Service of the Academy of Korean Studies (AKS-2015-OLU-2250005). I would also like to thank the Kim Chon-hung Fund at the University of Hawai'i Center for Korean Studies for supporting the publication of this book.

Note on Transliteration

The transliteration of Korean words follows the system of Korea's National Institute of Korean Language except for words and names that are usually transliterated in an alternative style in English-language literature. For Korean names, I generally put the given name first. The exceptions are well-known political figures such as Park Chung Hee, Kim Dae Jung, and Park Geun-hye.

PRIVILEGE AND ANXIETY

Introduction

THE FRACTURED MIDDLE

The dominant discourse on the middle class in most advanced economies is about its endangered status. Middle classes in many societies are steadily shrinking due to growing job market insecurity and dwindling incomes. The voluminous literature that has been produced on the contemporary middle classes often describes them as "squeezed," "shrinking," "hollowed out," or even "disappearing" (Birdsall, Graham, and Pettinato 2000; Garrett 2004; Pressman 2007; Leicht and Fitzgerald 2014; Milanovic 2016; OECD 2019). The dominant theme in this literature is clearly articulated in a recent publication by the Organisation for Economic Co-operation and Development (OECD) titled *Under Pressure: The Squeezed Middle Class* (2019):

> The middle class used to be an aspiration. For many generations it meant the assurance of living in a comfortable house and affording a rewarding lifestyle, thanks to a stable job with career opportunities. It was also a basis from which families aspired to an even better future for their children. However, there are now signs that this bedrock of our democracies and economic growth is not as stable as in the past.
>
> Middle incomes have barely grown, in both relative and absolute terms in many OECD countries; the cost of essential parts of the middle-class lifestyle has increased faster than income, notably housing and higher education; and job insecurity has risen in the context of fast transforming labour markets. Today, the middle class looks increasingly like a boat in rocky waters. (16)

This description fits the Korean situation. The country's middle class grew rapidly during the export-oriented industrialization of the latter half of the twentieth century. The remarkable economic growth produced a sharp rise in the number of white-collar workers and small business owners. Many people from the farming and laboring classes were able to move up into the middle class and could expect a better future for their children. By the time Korea hosted the Olympic Games in Seoul in 1988, the country was eager to present itself to the world as a nation of predominantly middle-class citizens. Indeed, according to many surveys conducted during that time, 70 percent of Koreans identified themselves as belonging to the middle class.

Less than a decade later, however, this auspicious trend was abruptly reversed with the onset of the Asian financial crisis in 1997. Koreans suffered many hardships, including a drastic rise of unemployment, massive layoffs, widespread bankruptcies, and negative economic growth. The crisis hit white-collar and managerial workers particularly hard. Many of them were laid off or forced to retire early and were unable to return to regular employment. Small business owners also suffered due to depressed consumer demand and increased competition as many of the newly unemployed sought to enter the small-business sector. While the Korean economy recovered fairly quickly, the woes of the working population have continued. During and after the financial crisis, Korea's labor market underwent a thoroughgoing neoliberal reform. Most large firms adopted a "flexibilization" approach that reduced the size of their workforce or transformed many of the remaining jobs from regular full-time employment to irregular or nonstandard employment. For most white-collar workers, lifetime employment became a thing of the past. The retirement age was lowered, and the possibility of layoffs remained a constant threat. The economic base of the middle class was thus severely damaged. By the 2010s, the number of people who felt they belonged to the middle class had fallen to around 40 percent of the population (see chapter 1), and the dominant discourse shifted from a rosy picture of an all middle-class society to dark tropes of middle-class doom and gloom.

But this is only part of the story of what happened to the Korean middle class during this period. If we look more closely, we find that different groups within this category had very different experiences. Obviously, the middle class does not represent a single homogeneous category. What happened during Korea's recent transition to a globalized economy was a sharp divergence in life experiences for the middle class between the economically successful minority and the majority. Diverging economic fortunes occurred in both the financial and labor markets. On the one hand, the financial crisis provided an excellent investment opportunity for cash-rich people to invest in the depressed real estate and stock markets in anticipation of a quick economic turnaround. Indeed, when the crisis ended after two years, a real estate boom and a bull stock market followed, and many people who were already doing well before the crisis came out of it even richer.

On the other hand, neoliberal structural reforms enacted during and after the financial crisis drastically changed the labor market. Many firms scratched the old seniority-based wage system and replaced it with a performance-based system, leading to widening wage differentials among salaried workers. The large conglomerates moved toward American-style management and began offering exceptionally high wages and stock options to a select cadre of professional and managerial employees. At the same time, an influx of transnational firms altered pay scales among Korean firms, elevating the salary levels for the top tier of managers especially those with global skills and experience. These shifts in corporate culture occurred in tandem with the Korean economy's gradual transition from labor-intensive to technology- and knowledge-based. The outcome of these changes was to greatly enhance the economic position of those who possessed the scarce skills demanded by the globalized economy.

All of these changes led to a spike in inequality in Korean society. This disparity has evolved in the form of economic polarization between those who were able to exploit the neoliberal transition of the economy and those who were unable to adapt due to a lack of resources. Of course, even in the past the middle class was not really homogeneous and had both rich and poor families. But in the old days the middle class was a relatively open and fluid category and allowed many middle-income people to become wealthy through hard work or entrepreneurial activities. Even if they did not become rich, ordinary Koreans generally felt that they were benefiting from the country's economic growth as much as most other people were. In contrast, today's nouveau riche have emerged in the midst of a deteriorating income situation for most income earners, which means that their rise is a consequence of income polarization rather than of overall income growth for all. In short, the new rich have emerged as the few winners in an economic system that has produced an abundance of losers.

The Objective of the Study

This book investigates how rising inequality in Korea brought internal division to the middle class, turning it into an arena of intense class distinction and status competition. As is well understood and well documented, neoliberal globalization has led to increasing inequality in most industrial societies. But most studies on this issue are interested in documenting the magnitude of economic inequality or explaining the causal aspects of this phenomenon. This is partly because the literature on this phenomenon is dominated by economists. My intention in this book is to extend this economic approach by integrating sociological concerns. The aim is to investigate how economic inequality is translated into social and cultural inequality and thereby promotes increasing competition for status and privilege within the middle class. The gap between segments of the middle class represents not simply economic disparity but also differential capacities to take advantage of the opportunities provided by the globalizing economy. The upper segment of the middle class is more closely integrated into the global system and has the wherewithal to acquire global cultural skills and cosmopolitan lifestyles. Hence, the upper middle class benefits from the globalized opportunity structure, while the less well-off are marginalized and disadvantaged by the same structure. Consequently, a middle class that used to be relatively homogeneous and fluid has slowly changed to an internally divided and socially fractured class.

Much of the new class dynamics occurring in the social space of the middle class is led by the affluent minority. Having emerged in an age of growing economic insecurity, this new group is eager to distinguish itself from less fortunate people and establish its privileged status. They seek class distinction through upscale consumption activities, residential segregation, and educational practices. Indeed, they lead better lives, living in larger houses or apartments and in nicer neighborhoods, enjoying a greater variety of more nutritious foods, and receiving better-quality health care. They embark on overseas travel more frequently and become familiar with other cultures and thereby obtain cosmopolitan cultural skills. Moreover, they can provide better, more competitive education for their children. With their similar economic status and similar lifestyles, these wealthier families tend to develop a sense of affinity among themselves. They are particularly keen to build social networks that can provide the types of information and personal connections that are useful for maintaining their position. They seek to distance themselves from others who could disturb their comfort or threaten their privileged status and do so both physically through residential segregation and socially through many subtle forms of class distinction. For all of these reasons, today's struggles for class distinction occur at the boundary between the affluent, privileged middle class and the ordinary middle class rather than at the traditional division between the middle class and the working class.

That this class differentiation is taking place in a rapidly globalizing economy is of special significance. Globalization has had a huge impact on class practices, especially among middle-class people. By "globalization," I refer primarily to economic rather than political, technological, or cultural globalization. As Steger (2009, 38) writes, "economic globalization refers to the intensification and stretching of economic interrelations across the globe. Gigantic flows of capital and technology have stimulated trade in goods and services. Markets have extended their reach around the world, in the process creating new linkages among national economies." Economic globalization allows today's affluent middle class to enjoy far more privileges than the wealthy of the past, thanks to all the goods and services provided by the global market and the relaxation of state control over luxury import consumption. During the preliberalization era, the state's tight control of the consumption market meant that the lifestyle of the wealthy was not all that different from that of the traditional middle class. Today, in contrast, the well-to-do can take full advantage of the many opportunities brought by globalization, including higher-quality consumer goods, well-being products that could improve their health, leisure trips abroad, global education for their children, world-class cultural activities, and retirement options in foreign countries. Moreover, globalization affects the stratification game by imposing new standards of competition and privileging certain skills and educational qualifications demanded by the globalized economy. Consequently, globalization inserts a wedge into the middle class that splits it into two groups: the small minority of winners who possess adequate material and human resources to benefit from the global system and the large majority of losers who lack adequate resources to adapt to the changing economic environment.

While those in the new affluent middle class appear to be winning the class distinction struggle, they cannot entirely escape its repercussions. Not surprisingly, those who have fallen behind are not inclined to simply give up. Class memory is an important factor for the losers, who remember quite clearly that the new rich used to be part of the middle class, just like themselves. Many middle-income people therefore take an active part in the escalating status game, driven by their anxiety not to be left behind and lose their middle-class status. Despite their unstable economic situation, they also enter the arena of conspicuous consumption and expensive private education for their children. Consequently, the middle class has become a social arena of intense status competition as its members either struggle for class privilege or simply struggle not to fall out of the middle class altogether. Gradually, the affluent middle class's lifestyle and social mobility strategies have come to define the desirable standards for respectable middle-class membership. In the meantime, the majority of the middle class who are struggling with precarious jobs and increasing family debts are becoming deeply frustrated and wonder whether they are still in the middle class.

Over the years the number of Koreans who identify themselves as belonging to the middle class declined drastically, from 70 to 80 percent in the 1990s to a low 40 percent in the late 2010s. In comparison, the number of people who are objectively classified as middle class by their income status declined more moderately, from 70 to 80 percent to a low of 60 percent during the same period. Such a large discrepancy between the objective and subjective identifications of the middle class suggests a growing confusion about the meaning of "middle class" in the minds of Koreans these days. This, I believe, is closely related to increasing economic differentiation occurring in the middle class.

Rise of the Affluent and Privileged

The rise of a new affluent and privileged minority as a separate stratum from the ordinary middle class began to receive serious attention in the United States in recent years. The rise of the "new middle class" or the "new rich" is of much interest to scholars working on the middle classes in the Third World but is discussed mainly in the context of the early stage of industrial development and the active role of the state (Robinson and Goodman 1996; Hsiao 1999, 2001; Pinches 1999; Tomba 2004; Fernandes 2006; Wang and Davis 2010; Heiman, Freeman, and Liechty 2012). In contrast, the debate on America's new elite groups is more directly relevant to my concern in this book, as it looks at this phenomenon in the context of the advanced stage of capitalism and the neoliberal transformation of the economy. It is thus useful to review a few key issues discussed in the American literature on the new wealthy segment of society.

In a provocatively titled essay in the *New York Times*, "Stop Pretending You're Not Rich," Richard Reeves (2017b) makes a strong argument that if we are concerned about economic polarization in America, we must redirect our attention from the upper 1 percent of income earners to those who are below it but still quite well-to-do. Reeves argues that the oft-used rhetoric of "the top 1 percent versus the bottom 99 percent" hides an important reality in America today, which is the rise of a small minority who are doing much better than the rest of the population in the current economy. The people he is referring to are those in the upper 10–20 percent income bracket. Reeves claims, both in the essay and in a book published the same year, *Dream Hoarders*, that "it is not just the 'upper class' that has been flourishing. A much broader swath of American society is doing well—and detaching themselves" (Reeves 2017a, 6). As he also points out, "The rhetoric of 'We are the 99 percent' has in fact been dangerously self-serving, allowing people with healthy six-figure incomes to convince themselves that they are somehow in the same economic boat as ordinary Americans" (Reeves 2017b).

The following year Matthew Stewart (2018) wrote an equally interesting article in *The Atlantic* titled "The 9.9 Percent Is the New American Aristocracy."

Stewart argues that "in between the top 0.1 percent and the bottom 90 percent is a group that has been doing just fine. It has held on to its share of a growing pie decade after decade.... You'll find the new aristocracy there. We are the 9.9 percent."

Reeves and Stewart use somewhat different cutoffs (the upper 10–20 percent versus the upper 9.9 percent) to identify their target group, but they both regard this group as constituting a new privileged class that is gradually separating from the ordinary middle class. As Stewart (2018) describes, "We 9.9 percenters live in safer neighborhoods, go to better schools, have shorter commutes, receive higher-quality health care, and, when circumstances require, serve time in better prisons. We also have more friends—the kind of friends who will introduce us to new clients or line up great internships for our kids."

Reeves (2017a) also emphasizes that the new upper middle class enjoys many privileges at the expense of other people because of "hoarding opportunities." Opportunity hoarding occurs in many ways, but he stresses three types: exclusionary zoning in residential areas; unfair mechanisms influencing college admissions, including legacy preferences; and the informal allocation of internships. Of the three, perhaps the most serious in America is zoning laws. Exclusionary zoning practices allow the upper middle class to live in enclaves or gated communities, even if the gates are not visible, with broad consequences. As Reeves (2017b) argues, "Since schools typically draw from their surrounding area, the physical separation of upper-middle–class neighborhoods is replicated in the classroom. Good schools make the area more desirable, further inflating the value of our houses. The federal tax system gives us a handout, through the mortgage-interest deduction, to help us purchase these pricey homes." In this way, wealth, residential segregation, tax deductions, and educational opportunities reinforce one another.

More recently, Daniel Markovits (2019) published *The Meritocracy Trap: How America's Foundational Myth Feeds Inequality, Dismantles the Middle Class, and Devours the Elite*. The book covers a new American elite, not the middle class, but has great relevance to the phenomenon this book covers because Markovits pays attention to the changing relations between the elite and the middle class. His main argument is that the meritocratic ideal—that social and economic rewards should be based on skills and achievement rather than breeding—has become almost like a civil religion in America and is a powerful force in shaping America's elite class and its relationship with the rest of society. This meritocracy has created a new elite, the "meritocratic elite," who are the best educated and trained. They work incredibly hard and long hours and in return receive unprecedented rewards. On the other side, "meritocracy banishes the majority of citizens to the margins of their own society, consigning middle-class children to lackluster schools and middle-class adults to dead-end jobs" (xiv). Thus, "meritocracy now divides the elite from the middle class" (x).

Markovits explains that the meritocratic elite is produced and maintained through two mechanisms. First, "meritocracy transforms education into a rigorous and intense contest to join the elite," and second, "meritocracy transforms work to create the immensely demanding and enormously lucrative jobs that sustain the elite" (Markovits 2019, 5). But who constitutes the meritocratic elite? Markovits suggests that it is composed of a core that captures about the top 1 percent of the national income and "a larger penumbra that works in the social and economic orbit of these incomes (perhaps another 5 or 10 percent)." In terms of occupational characteristics, the people he often refers to include executives at large corporations, hedge fund managers, specialist doctors, management consultants, partners at large law firms, and the like.

Another way to look at the newly emerged elite in America is to focus on its cultural aspects as a defining characteristic. In her book *The Sum of Small Things: A Theory of the Aspirational Class*, Elizabeth Currid-Halkett (2017) defines this new class as an "aspirational class" that aspires to separate itself from other classes not in terms of their economic status but instead through their lifestyle and cultural capital. "This new group is thus defined, more than anything else, through its shared cultural capital—they speak the same language, acquire similar bodies of knowledge, and share the same values, all of which embody their collective consciousness" (18). Class distinction occurs most clearly in the area of consumption, but Currid-Halkett stresses that today's rich are very different from Veblen's (1967) leisure class. "Because many conspicuous goods are now accessible to every income group, the wealthy do not distinguish themselves through goods that are widely available and increasingly affordable to the middle class" (Currid-Halkett 2017, 32). Instead, they spend a far larger proportion of their income on education and on goods and services that save time and provide a better quality of life. Thus, Currid-Halkett argues, "As showy and material means of establishing status are more accessible, the aspirational class finds subtle symbols, cultural capital, and language to distinguish itself from other groups, and its members use knowledge as an important dividing line between them and the rest" (51).

Almost three decades before any of these recent studies appeared, Barbara Ehrenreich (1989) presented a powerful analysis of America's elite middle class, which she calls "the professional and managerial middle class" or, for convenience, "the professional middle class." In *Fear of Falling: The Inner Life of the Middle Class*, Ehrenreich shows how this class segment changed from the early 1960s to the late 1980s in both their political consciousness and their relationship with other classes. From a relatively open, liberal, and inclusive group, the professional middle class gradually became closed, conservative, and selfish. She explains this in terms of changing self-identity as these people went from seeing themselves as part of a general middle class to believing they had a special status above that of ordinary people. "It was in this new and emerging self-consciousness *as an elite*," Ehrenreich writes, "that the middle class, or significant segments of it, turned right" (10).

Ehrenreich describes this change in the context of social and political dynamics that had evolved since the 1960s, but she recognizes that drastic economic changes that occurred in the 1980s had a powerful effect on the political character of the American professional middle class. The economic conditions for the majority of the middle class began to deteriorate, and inequality began to increase even among the middle class. Therefore, Ehrenreich writes, "The continued existence of the professional middle class, as a class, may eventually be in question. One chunk is moving up, perhaps to join en masse the corporate elite from whose hand it now securely feeds.... Meanwhile, another layer—less plucky or perhaps more stubbornly independent—sediments toward the white-collar end of the working class" (Ehrenreich 1989, 246). She saw the serious societal consequences of this internal division of the middle class. "So the nervous, uphill financial climb of the professional middle class accelerates the downward spiral of the society as a whole: toward cruelly widening inequalities, toward heightened estrangement along lines of class and race, and toward the moral anesthesia that estrangement requires" (250).

All these authors agree that the rise of a new stratum of affluent and privileged people above the mass middle class in America represents a new phenomenon that has developed since the mid-twentieth century. They do, however, vary in how they identify this new affluent segment of the population. Reeves and Stewart both identified the privileged groups in terms of their position in the income distribution. Even so, the authors chose different scales to select their subjects. Reeves defined his "upper middle class" as those in the upper 10–20 percent of income distribution, while Stewart selected a narrower group, the upper 9.9 percenters, and called them a "new aristocracy." Markovits, on the other hand, considered educational and occupational characteristics more important than income in defining his "meritocratic elite." Ehrenreich took a similar approach but emphasized education in defining the "professional and managerial middle class." Currid-Halkett is a little different from the others in selecting cultural capital and lifestyle as the defining criteria of the "aspirational class."

Most likely, this trend of class structural change is not limited to the United States but is somewhat common among advanced economies. A major study by British sociologists in recent years provides an illustrative case. Known as the

BBC's Great British Survey, this cross-national survey (with 161,000 respondents) was conducted in 2013 by a research team headed by Mike Savage, a prominent British sociologist. The report presents many illuminating findings, among which was the following: "Away from longstanding differences between middle and working class, we have moved towards a class order which is more hierarchical in differentiating the top (which we call 'the wealth elite') from the bottom (which we call 'the precariat' which consists of people who struggle to get by on a daily basis), but which is more fuzzy and complex in its middle layers" (Savage et al. 2015, 4).

The class landscape of Great Britain as described here seems very similar to that of the United States, that is, with polarization between the rich and the poor and an uneasy amalgamation of diverse groups as a middle class or middle classes. In more detail, Savage and his colleagues recognized two types of middle class: "the established middle class" and "the technical middle class." The upper class sits above these middle classes. It is worth noting that these authors define this upper class as the "wealth elite" or "new ordinary elite" rather than the "upper class." The traditional upper class still exists but represents only a very tiny group of decreasing social significance. Meanwhile, the new ordinary elite are growing in number and increasing their wealth and political influence. According to Savage et al.'s estimate, this new ordinary elite represents about 6 percent of the population (while the established middle class comprises about 25 percent) and is made up of people such as CEOs of large firms, financial managers, marketing and sales managers, and elite professionals. So, this new ordinary elite corresponds closely to Markovits's meritocratic elite. The British authors also emphasize meritocracy as a major social and cultural characteristic of their new ordinary elite.

Korea's Similarities and Differences

The rise of a new affluent group in Korea and its gradual separation from the ordinary middle class resemble the American and British patterns described in the previous section. As we will see more closely in chapter 2, Korea's income distribution since the 1990s has shown the same heavy concentration at the top, with the top 1 percent of the population experiencing a tremendous increase in their income. As in the United States and other advanced economies, Korea has also seen a significant increase in income among a broader segment (the upper 10–20 percent) of income earners below the super-rich, in contrast to stagnating income for the rest of the population. This income distribution pattern is markedly different from the pre-1990s trend. In the previous period, upper-, middle-, and lower-income groups all experienced the same steady income growth.

Also, as in America, growing economic disparity in Korea has led to widening social differentials in residential segregation, housing quality, consumption patterns, and lifestyles. The privileges available to the affluent in the consumer market have increased as the Korean economy has become more liberalized and globalized. With the wide opening of the Korean market to foreign imports, Korea's new rich can now spend their money on healthier and more luxurious and status-enhancing products than ever before. Their consumption patterns and lifestyles continue to be upgraded and separated from those of the lower middle class. Moreover, this class differential has come to be sharply expressed in the educational opportunities available to the different groups. Wealthy families can provide more competitive private education for their children from early on and can also send them overseas for global education as an alternative to the gruesome educational competition inside Korea.

Despite these similarities, there are several important differences in Korea compared to America and Great Britain in the ways the new affluent upper middle class has been formed. First, the rise of Korea's new affluent group, with its distinct lifestyle and mobility orientation, is a recent phenomenon. Its distinction from other middle-class members is a relatively new development that is evolving. Thus, the newly emerged wealthy Korean group, despite its many economic advantages, has not yet established a clear class identity compared to its American and British counterparts. Most of the Korean well-to-do feel they are still middle class. And while some of them are quite rich and no longer consider themselves middle class, they may not feel accepted as upper class either. Moreover, in the eyes of ordinary middle-class people, the new wealthy today are not so different from themselves in terms of their backgrounds, as most of the new rich used to be their former peers. When they cannot compete with the affluent group, those in the ordinary middle class naturally feel a great sense of relative deprivation. This is a major source of anxiety that is pervasive among Korean middle-class people today.

Second, the affluent middle-class people in Korea are similar to the new rich in other Asian countries in that they have accumulated wealth through speculative real estate investment and various forms of rent-seeking activity in the informal economy (Robison and Goodman 1996; Pinches 1999). This is related to Korea's political economy in which the state, often called a developmental state, has played a dominant role in allocating resources and devising the plans for the country's development. In the process of Korea's rapid economic growth, state-led industrial and urban development projects provided a major route for capital accumulation. It is well known that chaebol groups, which represent

Korea's upper class today, were largely created by favorable government policies. But below them, many financially alert and politically connected people have made tremendous profits from the booming real estate market. From the 1980s on, profits from real estate investment have constituted a major source of wealth for Korea's new rich. In fact, it can be said that Korea's upper middle class has been built through a series of real estate bubbles that occurred during the past two or three decades.

Third, for these reasons, the newly emergent affluent class has not been able to establish a superior moral or ideological position in society. Meritocracy is also an important value system in Korea. In fact, it is as old as Confucianism in Korea. But as long as the wealth accumulation strategy of the rich continues to be regarded with great suspicion, the new upper middle class is only an affluent and privileged class and cannot be called a meritocratic elite. Consequently, the new affluent middle class suffers a considerable amount of uneasiness and anxiety about its class identity. It is this status anxiety that encourages the new rich to engage in conspicuous consumption and a luxurious lifestyle in order to distinguish themselves from the ordinary middle class.

However, an important change has been occurring recently in the composition of the Korean upper middle class. With Korea's transition to a highly globalized economy that emphasizes knowledge- and technology-intensive industries, the number of high-level professional and managerial workers has increased. These professional and managerial workers have come to represent the affluent upper middle class, pushing aside those who made their money mainly through speculative real estate investment or other financial activities. With this change, the old image of the new rich, often called *jolbu* (vulgar rich), is slowly giving way to a new image of an educated elite. Today's corporate elite and professional workers are highly educated, many with postgraduate degrees from abroad, and work hard and intensely (no less than their American counterparts). They can therefore justify their class privilege in terms of meritocratic values of superior education, talent, and hard work. If this trend continues, as it most likely will, Korea's affluent middle class, or at least its upper segment, may be able to establish itself as a new meritocratic elite.

Fourth, globalization plays a far more important role in shaping the new privileged middle class in Korea than in America and other older advanced economies. Globalization is of course important for both advanced and newly industrialized societies, but it exerts a more powerful influence in the latter because their economies are newly integrated into global capitalism and therefore are subject to more changes driven by global forces. We have seen that Korea's aggressive embrace of globalization since the late 1990s has brought rising inequality and a new axis of division between those who adapt to global forces successfully and those who cannot. Globalization can thus be understood as an important causal factor for rising inequality and internal division within the middle class. In addition, globalization changes the context in which inequality is manifested by bringing new opportunities and new values to globalizing societies. It opens the doors to new consumer goods, new fashions and lifestyles, more freedom to travel abroad, increased opportunities for global education, and the like. In fact, these days the ability to participate actively in the globalized consumption and education markets is indicative of being in the privileged middle class. Their lifestyle and mobility strategies have become sharply distinguished from those who lack adequate resources to do the same, and this is why I regard the new affluent middle class as a "global middle class." In my previous writing, I defined the global middle class as "those who possess adequate economic and cultural resources to participate actively in the global market of consumption and education and seek social mobility and identity in the new global environment" (Koo 2016, 10).

My Approach

Considering all these factors, I call the newly emerged affluent segment of the middle class the "new upper middle class," or, alternatively, the "privileged middle class." The term "global middle class" is another appropriate term to be considered. But the term is more commonly used to refer to the newly emerged middle classes in the less developed economies than to the affluent segment of the middle class in advanced economies (Derne 2005; Parker 2009; Kharas and Gertz 2010; Kharas 2017). Also, in societies such as Korea where the impetus of globalization is so powerful that all members of the middle class have become globalized to a certain extent in their attitudes and behaviors, the terms "global" and "globalized" seem not to be particularly useful in distinguishing the affluent segment from the rest of the middle class.

As a rough estimate, I consider those in the upper 10 percent of the income hierarchy as belonging to Korea's new upper middle class today. In this sense, my conceptualization is similar to that of Reeves (2017a, 20–21), who sees the upper 10–20 percenters as constituting a "new upper middle class" in America. Of course, this group is not homogeneous. Many people in this category are not clearly differentiated from the mainstream middle class in terms of occupation or income. And some of them are much wealthier than most middle-class families and are close to the upper class. But as explained above, they are not really upper class either. It may make more sense to conceive of the wealthy segment of the professional and managerial workers as representing a separate category situated between the upper class and the middle class, as a "meritocratic elite" or "wealth elite." But I do not think these terms are particularly appropriate for Korea's new affluent group. As mentioned above, many of these people, professional or not, have accumulated their wealth through unearned income, such as speculative real estate investment and politically based rent-seeking activities. For this reason, the elements of meritocracy and elite are lacking in this group's class image as perceived by the public, though this may well change in the future.

The main concern of this book, however, is neither to name and classify nor to systematically analyze the privileged upper middle class. That is, my aim is not to provide a narrowly focused sociological analysis of any particular class. Rather, my interest is in investigating the social and cultural processes brought by rising inequality in the social space of the middle. The affluent middle class plays a particularly important role in these processes and therefore deserves close attention. But if we focus too narrowly on this class, we may lose sight of the larger processes occurring in the whole society. Therefore, my study aims to analyze class relations and class processes rather than the static class structure.

In fact, my approach represents a new sociological orientation to studying the middle class as well as other classes. Influenced by a cultural turn in sociology, the new scholarship on the middle class likes to conceive of class as a historical and cultural process. As Wacquant (1991, 39–40) argues, "The boundary of the middle class . . . cannot be adequately addressed at an abstract theoretical level and should thus be tackled, if at all, through historical analysis." He further writes that "political and symbolic factors necessarily play a crucial role in the constitution of the middle class (and of any class, for that matter)" (51). Similarly, Liechty (2003, 16), in his incisive study of the Nepali middle class, argues that "the middle class is a constantly renegotiated cultural space—a space of ideas, values, goods, practices, and embodied behaviors—in which the terms of inclusion and exclusion are endlessly tested, negotiated, and affirmed. From this point of view, it is the process, not the product, that constitutes class."

In a similar fashion, I approach the middle class not as a fixed category but instead as a fluid and somewhat fuzzy collectivity of individuals and families occupying a broadly similar economic position in the middle of the society. In taking this approach, I subscribe to Bourdieu's conception of class as "social space" whereby class positions are defined by three forms of capital: economic, social, and cultural. More specifically, Bourdieu (1984, 114) argues that class represents "a space whose three fundamental dimensions are defined by volume of capital, composition of capital, and change in these two properties over time (manifested by past and potential trajectory in social space)." He explicates how class interests and dispositions are shaped by these factors: "constructed classes can be characterized in a certain way as sets of agents who, by virtue of the fact that they occupy similar positions in social space (that is, in the distribution of powers), are subject to similar conditions of existence and conditioning factors and, as a result, are endowed with similar dispositions which prompt them to develop similar practices" (Bourdieu 1987, 6). A big advantage of considering class as a social space rather than a fixed structural category is that doing so allows us to avoid becoming preoccupied with determining objective criteria of class membership or class boundaries and instead pay more attention to the flux of social processes that essentially make up any class.

Organization of the Book

Chapter 1 provides the background of the rise of the Korean middle class in the era of rapid economic growth (from the early 1960s to the 1980s) and its sudden decline since the late 1990s. A product of state-driven export-oriented industrialization, middle-class formation in Korea has been shaped by the state's political and ideological objectives as much as economic change. The state was deeply interested in fostering the middle class as a vanguard of modernization and used this class to showcase Korea's economic miracle. The middle class was thus conceptualized in very loose economic terms to make it easier for many people to identify themselves as belonging to it. The middle class had expanded vigorously thanks to rapid economic growth but began to decline after the 1997 Asian financial crisis. However, the causes of this middle-class breakdown are more than economic. Social and psychological factors have played just as important a role, as demonstrated by the subjective identification with the middle class dropping more drastically than the actual change in economic conditions.

Chapter 2 investigates the rising inequality and the patterns of economic polarization that have become apparent since the financial crisis. The analysis focuses on two different forms of polarization: one occurring horizontally between regularly employed and non–regularly employed workers and between employees of large firms and smaller firms and the other occurring vertically between a minority of top income earners and the rest of the population. The data indicate that the recent neoliberal economic reform brought a huge income gain at the very top (the top 1 percent) and declining income for the middle-income groups. The data also indicate that the upper 10–20 percent of income earners have seen their income grow substantially as well. Because many of those in this income category can be considered to belong to the middle class rather than the upper class, this finding suggests an important division occurring within the middle class. The evidence also suggests that the boundary between the upper middle class and the ordinary middle class has become more important than a traditional division between manual and nonmanual workers or between the working class and the middle class.

The most visible way class distinction and status competition unfold in modern societies is through consumption. Chapter 3 investigates how growing inequality in Korea has manifested itself in the arena of consumption and lifestyle and describes how the new rich strive to distance themselves from the ordinary middle class through conspicuous consumption of luxury goods and maintaining a trendy lifestyle. Prior to the 1980s the Korean consumption market was relatively underdeveloped, and consumption played a less crucial role in determining one's status. This was due not just to the still-modest incomes of the middle class but also to the tight control the state maintained over people's consumption behavior. But consumption patterns started to change noticeably as the Korean economy began to open to consumer imports from the early 1980s. As Korea became a full-fledged consumer society in the 1990s, widening economic gaps within the middle class led to social and cultural forms of class distinction, primarily through conspicuous consumption. It was the new rich who led this trend, consuming various kinds of luxury brand-name products imported from the West. Then, luxury consumption spread to the lower-income groups and boosted their imitative consumption, with adverse effects on their already precarious economic situation.

Related to consumption, another important form of class distinction that has developed in Korea since the 1980s is spatial segregation by class. Korea's residential patterns drastically changed with the development of Gangnam, the area of Seoul to the south of the Han River. Chapter 4 looks at the rise of Gangnam and examines its implications for the changing contours of the Korean class structure. The emergence of this affluent middle-class area with its own peculiar class culture makes it difficult to understand Korea's changing class dynamics without considering Gangnam's special significance. Gangnam is widely known for its high fashion and luxury consumption as well as its privileged educational opportunities. The dense congregation of good schools and top-rated private educational facilities (*hagwon*) led to real estate prices rising continuously at a much faster rate than in other urban areas. Thus, Gangnam and its residents are often viewed with a mix of envy, jealousy, and resentment. Entering the new century, Gangnam's real estate prices became so high that middle-income families residing in other areas now find it almost impossible to move into the area. Gradually, a class boundary has been drawn between Gangnam and non-Gangnam areas, and Gangnam (at least its core districts) is increasingly the exclusive province of economically successful people. For many upwardly oriented middle-class people, the Gangnam lifestyle is the model of success that, however, is highly materialistic, conspicuous, and competitive. In short, Gangnam's development has contributed to the sharpening of a class boundary between the upper middle class and the ordinary middle class.

Because of the importance of education for the middle class, the next two chapters are devoted to this issue. Chapter 5 explores why the Korean educational system, which is widely regarded as one of the best in the world, is a source of so much frustration and anxiety for Koreans and why in recent decades it has ceased to function as a ladder of upward social mobility for most people. The most significant aspect of educational development in Korea in the past few decades has been the expansion of supplementary private education (or cram schools) and its dominance over the public educational system. I interpret this phenomenon in terms of the growing power of the upper middle class vis-à-vis the egalitarian state. Affluent middle-class families strongly resisted the state's attempt to create an egalitarian high school system and chose to seek after-school private education in order to give their children an edge in their quest for elite college admission. The consequence of this class resistance was the abnormal expansion of the private education industry. As time went by, private supplementary education became more important than public school education in determining students' chances of landing a place at elite universities. This means that their parents' financial resources have become more important than the children's own effort and talent. The concentration of first-rate cram schools and other private institutions in Gangnam has made class influences on students' educational success even more pernicious.

Chapter 6 pays closer attention to the global dimension of education. With Korea's aggressive pursuit of economic globalization, many changes have occurred in the educational system, including the rise of English as an essential skill and the increasing trend of Korean students going abroad to acquire more marketable educational qualifications. Those in the professional and managerial class adapted most swiftly to this change. They started a new trend of early study abroad for their children, often accompanied by the mothers (forming the so-called wild geese families). This strategy is used for both domestic and overseas purposes. Domestically, early study abroad allows a child to spend a couple of years in America or another English-speaking country and come back to Korea with greatly improved English skills, which is a tremendous advantage in the competition for admission to an elite school (high school or college) in Korea. Alternatively, a child may stay abroad for college. This is a good option for children who possess special talents or academic interests that could be cultivated better at elite universities in America or Europe than in Korea. But this strategy is more often used as a means to avoid downward mobility if a child is not doing well in the Korean school system. In many ways, the expansion of the global education market increases the advantages of the privileged middle class while consolidating the disadvantages of the less well-off. But the constantly changing educational game in the globalized world leaves no group free of uncertainty and anxiety.

In the concluding chapter I summarize the major findings and arguments in the book and discuss their sociological implications. The conclusion also explains the relevance of the book's findings to other societies and how my approach benefited from Bourdieu's theory of class distinction but also departed from it in some important aspects.

1

THE RISE AND FALL OF THE KOREAN MIDDLE CLASS

In her 2012 presidential election campaign, Park Geun-hye pledged to restore the shrinking middle class to 70 percent of the population. This is how large Koreans believed the country's middle class was in the late 1980s, thanks to the rapid economic growth promoted by her late father, Park Chung Hee. But Korea has experienced a drastic decline of its middle class since the Asian financial crisis in the late 1990s. How to halt the decline of the middle class and restore its vitality has thus become a dominant political and economic agenda in recent decades. While other political parties also campaigned to protect the ailing middle class, Park Geun-hye's catchy slogan is widely believed to have greatly assisted her electoral success.

Unfortunately, Park Geun-hye did little to reverse the downward slide of the middle class before her impeachment due to political mismanagement and corruption charges. Nevertheless, her successful presidential campaign demonstrated how much significance Koreans attach to the size of the middle class as a barometer of social progress and good governance.

The Rise of the Middle Class

The rise of the middle class in Korea was a direct consequence of the rapid industrial development in the last decades of the twentieth century. Prior to embarking on its export-oriented industrialization project in the early 1960s, Korea was predominantly an agrarian society with the majority of its population living and working on the farm. It is true that Korea experienced substantial industrial development during the Japanese colonial period and saw the growth of a small group of lower-level bureaucrats, teachers, bank clerks, and underemployed intellectuals. While this group could be regarded as the first modern middle class in Korea, its very small size and peculiar character of being entirely dependent on the colonial government makes the label an uneasy fit.

The rapid industrialization that began in the 1960s, however, brought about radical changes in the economy and in the ways people worked and made a living. The occupational shift was striking: in the late 1950s, four-fifths of the total Korean labor force consisted of agricultural workers, most of whom were small owner-cultivators. By the early 1980s the agricultural labor force was only one-third of the total labor force, and by the late 1990s only one out of ten working people remained on the farm. Thus, in the span of three decades, a nation of small cultivators became a nation of urban wage workers. This is clearly a case of "compressed modernity," as aptly described by Chang Kyung-Sup (2010).

The rise of the middle class is well reflected in Korea's occupational structural change from the 1960s through the 1990s. According to data provided by the Korean Statistical Association, the category of professional, managerial, and technical workers comprised only 2.9 percent of the total workforce in 1965 but increased to 10 percent in 1992. The number of ordinary white-collar workers more than tripled, from 4.1 percent to 14.4 percent, during the same period. Altogether, what might be broadly categorized as the "new middle class" increased from 7 percent to 24.4 percent between the mid-1960s and the early 1990s. By 1997, the new middle class had grown to about 30 percent of the labor force. Also notable is the significant increase of service and sales workers from 18.4 percent to 29.3 percent between 1965 and 1992. This category is composed of highly heterogeneous groups, some of whom would belong to what sociologists call the old middle class or the petite bourgeoisie, while others would be part of the urban marginal class. About half of those in the sales and service category could be considered as belonging to the middle class. They represented 11.5 percent of the workforce in 1997. Thus, the entire middle class (new and old), as measured by occupational distribution, was estimated to be about 42 percent of the population in 1997.

Chungsancheung as the Middle Class

In conceptualizing the Korean middle class, both scholars and media experts have avoided a Marxist terminology and instead have chosen to use a bland stratification term, *chungsancheung*. The term indicates middle-property strata or middle-income groups.[1] The selection of this term was primarily motivated by politics to avoid any ideological suspicion from the staunchly anticommunist state. But it also made sense to ordinary people who just climbed out of poverty and were eager to achieve an economically secure and comfortable life. *Chungsancheung* includes a diverse group of people engaged in diverse occupations, from professional and managerial workers, civil servants, and many private-sector white-collar workers to small business owners, taxi drivers, skilled mechanics, and the like. The job market was growing fast, and opportunities to earn a decent income were opening up everywhere. Many people began to feel that their economic lot was much better than that of their parents and looked forward to a better future. *Chungsancheung* provided a handy social identity that many people could relate to or aspire to achieve in the near future.

Despite its widespread use, the *chungsancheung* concept was rarely defined in any precise terms. In a major social survey conducted by Seoul National University sociologists in 1987, *chungsancheung* was defined as "those who are not necessarily rich but economically comfortable enough to send their children to college, maintain social relationships with others at a socially respectable standard, be able to take a family summer vacation trip, and enjoy a certain level of cultural life" (Han, Kwon, and Hong 1987). Similarly, the author of the book *Are You Chungsancheung* defines *chungsancheung* as those who are able to maintain a "respectable level of living standard" (Lee 1980). By the "respectable level," he meant the "financial ability to send children to advanced schools, maintain social relationships at least at face-saving level, and, by stretching a bit, to participate occasionally in cultural activities." Both definitions suggest that *chungsancheung* is basically an economic concept, defined in terms of having adequate income to possess one's own housing, provide a good education to children, and participate in consumption activities at the level appropriate to average citizens in a society.

Defined in this rather imprecise and inclusive sense, *chungsancheung* thus provided a convenient concept with which Koreans could interpret their situation in the period of rapid economic growth. Becoming part of the middle class was an important criterion of social success for most ordinary people. By the 1980s, a majority of Koreans could compare their lives to that of their parents' or even their own lives in the recent past and see the substantial improvement in their living standards and look forward to further improvement. Vague as it is, the *chungsancheung* notion represented this widespread subjective sense of economic improvement and upward social mobility. It also contained an optimistic future orientation for oneself and for one's children. In this regard, the middle class can be understood as an "aspirational category." In fact, such a notion of the middle class is not unique to Korea. As Schielke (2012, 40), referring to the Egyptian middle class, writes, "The middle class, more than any other class, is oriented toward the future. It is less about being than it is about becoming, about aspiration to a place, so to speak, in the middle of the society as a respectable person in relative comfort and with an optimistic future."

Chungsancheung as a Discourse and a Social Contract

But the formation of the middle class in Korea, as elsewhere, was not the product of economic factors alone. It was also a product of symbolic processes involving ideology, discourse, and cultural representation (Bourdieu 1984, 1987; Wacquant 1991; Fernandes 2006). In Korea, a state-sponsored political discourse played a particularly important role in shaping the middle class. Having come to power through a military coup, the Park Chung Hee regime (1961–1979) sought to establish its political legitimacy by delivering rapid economic growth. Making the nation strong and prosperous and raising the standard of living for the population was the overriding goal of the government, which nicely translated into the project of building a middle-class society. The ultimate goal of the nation, Park claimed, was to achieve *jokuk keundaehwa* (modernization of the fatherland) and to remold itself into *seonjin han'guk* (advanced-nation Korea). The rapidly growing number of middle-class people was thus taken as a visible sign of successful economic growth as well as a vindication of the choices that had been made to speed the nation on its path to modernization. The most popular slogans promoted by the Park government and echoed throughout society were *jalsala bose* (let's achieve a better life) and *hamyon doenda* (we can do it). Park Chung Hee promised to bring a my-car society by the end of the 1970s, a society where the majority of Koreans would be enjoying the middle-class life. The middle-class discourse thus served as a critical means for the Park government to consolidate its political legitimacy both inside and outside the country. As Yang (2012, 425) aptly explains, "the rise of the middle class was an important political-ideological project for the Korean state, one that sought to showcase its economic modernization to the world and legitimize state developmental projects." Of course, Korea was not unique in using the middle class as an important political discourse. This has been a common practice in state-led development processes in East Asia. For example, as David Goodman (2014, 116) argues in the context of China, "The state-sponsored discourse of the middle class plays an important role in the PRC [People's Republic of China]. It is designed to encourage consumption and hard work. It is intended to be inclusive, drawing attention away from the extremes of inequality and potential class conflict."

Another important aspect of *chungsancheung* in Korea is its role as a social contract. The idea that the middle class serves as the main basis of the social contract in advanced societies is well recognized among social scientists (see Zunz, Shoppa, and Hiwatari 2002). As Zunz (2002, 2) argues, "The social contracts of the postwar years stimulated middle-class expansion in the advanced industrialized nations, dramatically accelerating the American prewar trend of merging the working and middle classes into a huge, albeit differentiated middle class." In Korea, the social contract was implicitly made between the developmental state and individual citizens. This contract involved a shared assumption that people would be rewarded for working hard and cooperating with the state's development goals. The state demanded that individuals work hard, exercise self-discipline, comply with their employers, and defer political freedom and democracy. In return, the state promised to improve their living standards further and help them join the respectable middle class. By and large, it was a fair exchange for white-collar workers but not for blue-collar industrial workers. The factory workers were severely exploited in the low-paying, harsh working conditions, and their demands for justice in the workplace had been brutally crushed all along until the mass labor revolt erupted in the late 1980s (Koo 2001). Yet, the *chungsancheung* ideology was powerful enough to mobilize the whole population for hard work and dedication to the state's developmental project.

Middle-Class Identity

In the 1960s, Japan boasted of its "90 percent middle-class" or "all one hundred million middle-class society" (*ichioku sou-churyu shakai*).[2] Korean leaders aspired to bring Korea to the same stage by the end of the 1980s. Indeed, by the time of the 1998 Olympic Games in Seoul, Korea seemed to have achieved its middle-class goal. Many newspapers reported survey findings indicating that 70 percent or more of Koreans regarded themselves as middle class in the late 1980s. The percentage rose even higher in the first half of the 1990s, as found in numerous surveys conducted by newspapers, research organizations, and academic researchers.[3] Despite a large variation among survey findings, the general pattern was clearly a continuous increase in the share of people who considered themselves *chungsancheung*: from around 40 percent in the 1960s to about 60 percent in the 1970s, 60–70 percent in the 1980s, and eventually 70–80 percent in the late 1980s and the 1990s (see Hong 2005).

Now, an interesting question is what Koreans had in mind when they were asked whether they were *chungsancheung*. In other words, what criteria did they use when identifying one's own or somebody else's status as *chungsancheung*? This question was explored in several surveys. One survey conducted by Ehwa Womans University sociologists in 1999 asked the respondents what they had in mind when judging people as belonging or not belonging to *chungsancheung* (see Ham, Lee, and Park 2001). The respondents were allowed to select multiple factors. The results showed that an absolute majority (83%) of the respondents who considered themselves *chungsancheung* selected "stable income and economic comfort" as the number one factor in determining their status. All other factors, such as "occupational characteristics," "cultural and leisure activities," and "political attitudes or social participation," were selected by less than 10 percent. Another survey, conducted by Doo-Seung Hong in 2002, found basically the same pattern. The respondents were asked to select the two items they considered most important in identifying *chungsancheung*. The order of their selections was income status (79.5%), consumption standard (43.0%), cultural-leisure life (22.1%), occupational status (21.5%), education (17.2%), healthy value system (12.3%), civic participation (3.3%), and political attitude (0.7%) (Hong 2005, 114).

Thus, it is obvious that Koreans have had a very economistic conception of the middle class. This is not especially surprising, considering that so much societal attention had been given to the goal of becoming rich (*jalsala bose*) and the way *chungsancheung* had been framed in the media primarily as a consumption class. Nevertheless, it is somewhat puzzling that the survey respondents gave so little attention to social and cultural aspects in defining the middle class. All these surveys show that the respondents regarded moral and cultural aspects the least important in determining a person's class position. Of course, this would not necessarily mean that Koreans do not value moral and cultural aspects in evaluating other persons; rather, it indicates that moral and cultural values seem to be largely irrelevant in distinguishing one class from another. Presumably, the middle class was—and still is—regarded as a group of people who have more money and enjoy a more comfortable lifestyle but are not necessarily more honest, trustworthy, or civic-minded than other people.

In this regard, the Korean middle class is quite different from the prototypical middle class that is portrayed in the literature on the early European and American middle classes in the nineteenth century. As well documented in many historical studies, the nineteenth-century middle classes in Europe claimed their class identities on the basis of certain moral and religious values rather than simple economic possession. As Davidoff and Hall (1987, 450) write about the British middle class, "From the late eighteenth century, serious middle-class people increasingly claimed moral power for themselves, a claim fueled by religious belief and the 'proud pretensions' of those who relied on heavenly approbation rather than earthly spoils. Their rejection of landed wealth as the source of honour and insistence on the primacy of the inner spirit brought with it a preoccupation with the domestic as a necessary basis for a good Christian life."

Beyond this religious devotion, early European middle classes developed their distinct value system and tried to distinguish themselves from other classes on the basis of moral and cultural qualities. As Frykman and Löfgren (1987, 266) describe, "the bourgeoisie defined itself as a class that was fit to lead because of its many virtues: its high moral standards, its self-discipline and moderation, its thrift and rationality, its firm belief in science and progress. The classes above and below were felt to lack these qualities." The American middle class revealed the same cultural values and domestic practices. As Blumin (1989, 188) indicates, American middle-class families in the nineteenth century made "a deliberate attempt to shape the domestic environment in ways that signified social respectability and that facilitated the acquisition of habits of personal deportment that could set a family apart from both the rough world of the mechanics and the artificial world of fashion." It is very clear that both in Europe and America, middle-class people regarded cultural and moral values as being far more important than wealth or power in determining class status.

Today's middle classes in Europe and America are, of course, very different from their predecessors. As we know well, the middle classes today are far less religious and moralistic, and their value system puts more emphasis on wealth and material possession as the basis of social status. Yet, it is possible that the earlier middle-class values may not have completely disappeared and continue to influence the self identity and class behaviors among the European and American middle classes. A well-known study of the French and American middle classes by Lamont (1992) found interesting differences in the ways these two countries' upper middle- class people draw symbolic boundaries between themselves and those they have low regard for. The French upper middle-class men tend to emphasize cultural sophistication, intelligence, and sophisticated manners, while their American counterpart regard moral qualities such as honesty, personal integrity, and consideration of others more important. But what is common in the two countries is the fact that the upper middle-class people put more emphasis on cultural and moral qualities than economic possession or worldly success as a qualification of respectable people. A more recent study of the upper middle class in New York (Sherman 2017) describes a great deal of anxiety experienced among the wealthy concerning their class position. Sherman's in-depth interviews of New York's affluent people reveal that many of them feel uncomfortable about being rich in a highly unequal society. Conscious of the advantages they enjoy, these wealthy people defend themselves by emphasizing that they spend money modestly and prudently, try to give back to society, and raise children with good values in a non-materialistic way. Although one could wonder whether we must take what they say at face value, it seems obvious that affluent Americans have a strong desire to be taken as morally worthy people, not just as wealthy and successful people. I believe such a strong moral concern is much weaker among the new rich in Korea, which may be the same in most other newly industrialized economies.

The reasons, I believe, are less to do with differences in national cultures than with different historical contexts in which the middle classes emerged in the First World and the Third World. The early European middle classes emerged in a unique historical context of early modernization, the Enlightenment movement, and the evangelical religious movement. The middle classes were a critical agent of modernity during this period (López and Weinstein 2012). The Korean middle class—and, more broadly, "the global middle class" that appeared in the late twentieth century—was deprived of such a historical role. By this time, modernity had been established already in the First World, and the role of the middle class in developing countries was simply to borrow or copy the Western model. The idea of modernity and the image of the middle class itself had to be imported from the First World, more specifically from the United States in the case of South Korea.[4] The dominant culture in today's late capitalism is represented by materialism, consumerism, and globalism.

Not surprisingly, the Korean middle, being born without a historical mission to play a genuine role of modernizer and being shaped by the powerful force of global consumerism, has been molded primarily in a materialistic and consumeristic fashion. In fact, Korea had additional factors that contributed to shaping the middle class in that direction. One is the state's ideology of developmentalism, which put economic growth above any other goals of the nation and encouraged people to march under the slogans of *jalsala bose* and *hamyon doenda*. Becoming rich was regarded as a prime virtue for the individuals in this materialistic environment. Thus, the claims of middle-class status were made primarily on the basis of the economic and materialistic criteria above anything else. The media actively collaborated with the state in promoting this materialistic orientation of the people by constantly highlighting all the consumerist images of "happy middle-class life" borrowed from America and Europe.

A Sudden Reversal

In 1996, the monthly magazine *Shin Dong-A* conducted an opinion survey on the quality of life in Korea. The findings were amazingly positive. "Two out of three Koreans answered they were happy. One out of three believed they were living better than others, and two-thirds thought they lived as well as others and believed their life would be better in the future." And eight out of ten respondents believed they were middle class in terms of their living standards. So, the magazine concluded, "Koreans are happy and optimistic people" (*Shin Dong-A*, January 1996).

It is remarkable that this kind of optimistic picture of Korean society was expressed only one year before the arrival of the horrendous financial crisis in 1997. The Asian financial crisis is widely recognized as a major turning point in the South Korean economy and in the fortunes of the Korean middle class. The most serious consequence of this economic crisis was a sharp rise in unemployment. The number of jobless workers tripled from 658,000 in December 1997 to 1.7 million in December 1998. The majority of those who lost their jobs were manual laborers. But a significant proportion of those laid off were white-collar and managerial workers. A large number of layoffs occurred in the financial sector, as many banks collapsed or merged into bigger banks. It was reported that about 10 percent of the employees of the five largest conglomerate (chaebol) groups lost their jobs (Shin and Chang 2000). Many managerial workers in their forties and fifties were forced to retire early, taking so-called "honorary retirement."

All these economic troubles were a serious blow to the Korean middle class. It was in this gloomy economy that the "collapse," "downfall," or "demise" of the middle class became a dominant public discourse, echoed frequently by the media, politicians, and academics. Hardly any major newspaper failed to feature special coverage on the collapse of the Korean middle class during this period. According to a survey conducted by the Hyundai Research Institute in 1999, only 45 percent of the respondents considered themselves *chungsancheung*, a sharp drop from the 70 percent of only a few years before (HRI 1999).

From the 1990s the Korean government's statistical office, Statistics Korea, began to define the middle class according to the popular OECD measure as those earning 50 percent to 150 percent of median income. So, the government could collect consistent data on the changing proportion of Korea's middle class from the early 1990s. The data presented in figure 1.1 demonstrate that Korea's middle class decreased from 74.8 percent in 1990 to 70.2 percent in 2000 and to 65.4 percent in 2010 and remained there until 2015. Compared to other advanced economies, Korea experienced a substantially faster rate of middle-class decline over the past two or three decades. According to a recent OECD report, proportions of middle-income households in OECD countries fell, on average, from 64 percent to 61 percent between the mid-1980s and mid-2010s (OECD 2019).

But the decreasing share of the middle class in Korea is more sharply revealed when measured in terms of subjective identification of the individuals rather

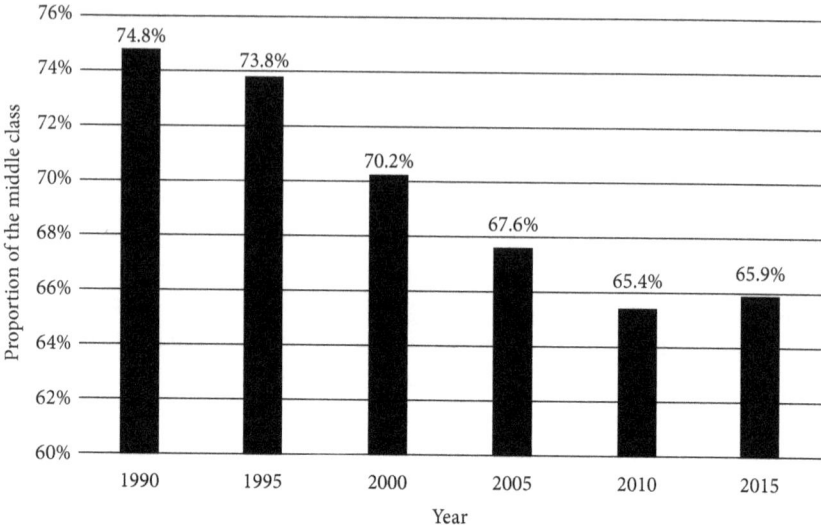

FIGURE 1.1. The proportion of the middle class (measured as those earning 50% to 150% of the median income)

Note: Data are based on urban households of two or more members.
Source: Yoon et al. (2014), KOSIS (2017).

than objective income status. Subjective identification as *chungsancheung* fell to mid-40 percent at the end of the 1990s. It recovered a little after the crisis but then began to decline again from the early 2000s. In a survey conducted by the *JoongAng Daily* in the winter of 2005, 56 percent of the respondents said they considered themselves *chungsancheung* (JoongAng Daily 2006). This is "an unprecedented decline," the report says, comparing this figure to the 70 percent found by the same survey in 1994 (see figure 1.2). Another major newspaper, the *Chosun Daily*, conducted a large-scale survey in 2019 and found that 48.7 percent of the respondents identified their class position as *chungsancheung* (Park 2019). An equal number of respondents (48.9%) said they belonged to the low-income class, while only 2.4 percent placed themselves in the high-income class (see figure 1.2). Still another survey conducted by the newspaper *Maeil Kyungje* found 42.2 percent of the respondents identifying themselves as *chungsancheung* (Kim and Park 2019).

Whether measured by objective income criteria or subjective criteria of self-identification, it is obvious that the Korean middle class has been shrinking significantly since the mid-1990s. What is behind this continuous decline of the Korean middle class? The answers are not difficult to find. In fact, in the literature there is wide agreement about the causal factors.

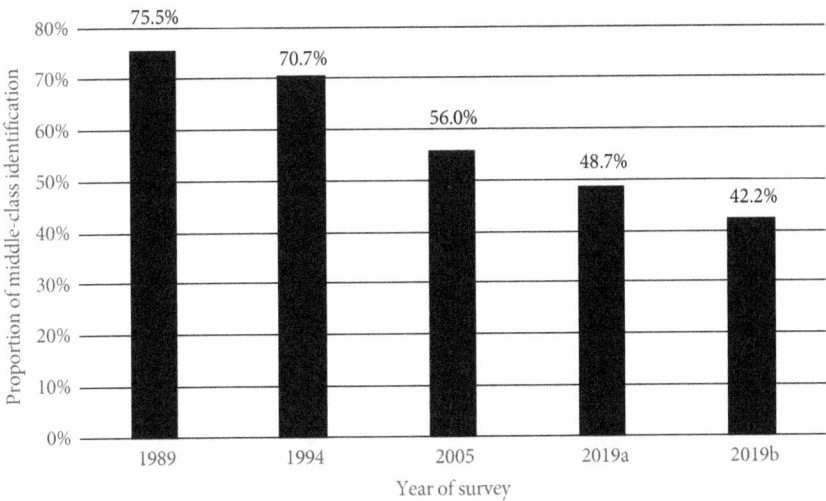

FIGURE 1.2. Subjective middle-class identification

Source: JoongAng Daily (2006), Kim and Park (2019), Park (2019).

The first and foremost reason is job market insecurity, which means reduced and unstable income sources. As the Korean economy has become neoliberalized and digitalized since the late 1990s, the job market for the middle class has become increasingly insecure and precarious. Many large firms have adopted a flexible labor market approach and reduced the number of new hires, while replacing many routine white-collar jobs with automation.[5] And many jobs in both large and medium-sized firms have changed from regular standard employment to a nonstandard form of employment with no fixed contracts. Even for regular workers, the retirement age has been lowered substantially in all large firms. One study indicated that the average retirement age for managerial workers in large firms was fifty-three in the 2010s (Shin 2015). At that age, many retirees still have children who are attending school and need to be supported for at least a few more years. So, many retirees must seek temporary or unstable jobs or self-employment, which typically involves downward mobility from managerial positions to marginal middle-class or lower-class positions.

On top of the parents' job instability, the younger generation faces a tough time finding stable jobs. Over the years the number of good jobs has hardly grown, while the number of college graduates has greatly increased due to the expansion of college enrollment since the 1990s. It is thus rather common among many new college graduates to spend two to three years holding temporary jobs before landing a stable career job. Sadly, the millennials, who represent the best-educated generation in Korea, find the grimmest job market waiting for them when they graduate from college.

It is this combination of parents' and children's job market troubles within the same household that makes it difficult for many middle-income families to maintain their *chungsancheung* status. As Shin (2015, 68) argues, "The sense of crisis deepens among middle-class households, as the difficulties of the parents' generation owing to an early retirement age are combined with the inability of the children's generation to obtain middle-class jobs and income despite their high educational achievements."[6]

Apart from job market problems, another serious cause of the middle-class decline is the rising cost of housing, education, medical care, and consumer goods and services in general. That means, while incomes have stagnated, it has become more expensive to maintain middle-class living standards. Of course, this is not a unique problem in Korea but rather common in most advanced economies. In OECD countries, for example, housing prices have grown on average three times faster than household median income over the last two decades (OECD 2019). In Korea, housing prices have increased twofold while average income has grown 33 percent over the past three decades; that is, the cost of housing has grown six times faster than income (Kim and Park 2019). In Korea, educational costs are no less serious a burden than housing costs. The average middle-class family spent 6.8 percent of their disposable income on the children's education in 2000 and 10.5 percent in 2013 (HRI 2015). Indeed, rising educational costs are regarded as their number one problem by most middle-class families (HRI 2015; Hong 2005).

In addition to labor market insecurity and the rising cost of maintaining a middle-class lifestyle, some demographic factors also contributed to the shrinking size of the middle class. One is the aging of the population, and another is the growth of single-person households. In the twentieth century, Korea has become one of the most aged societies in the world. Unlike in advanced economies with well-developed social security systems, Korea has not yet developed a decent welfare system for the elderly population. Thus, once they retire from white-collar jobs, most middle-class people become vulnerable to downward mobility. The rise of single-person households is another important demographic trend that contributes to the weakening of the middle class, because a large proportion of single people do not earn an adequate income to maintain a middle-class lifestyle. As in other advanced economies, maintaining middle-class standards in today's Korean society normally requires both incomes of a double-income couple.[7]

The Changing Meaning of *Chungsancheung*

The decline of the Korean middle class has been observed in terms of both objective measure and subjective identification. Yet this change is shown more dramatically in the number of people who identify themselves as middle class than in the share of people who are in the middle-income category. As we have seen, the middle class, defined by its income status (50–150% of median income), declined from 75 percent in the mid-1990s to 58 percent in 2019. But the number of people who regard themselves as belonging to *chungsancheung* dropped from about 70–80 percent in the mid-1990s to 40–50 percent in 2019. In fact, another survey conducted in 2013 by the Korean Sociological Association found that only 20.2 percent of the respondents regarded themselves as *chungsancheung* (Yee 2014).

These findings suggest that many people whose income levels would make them middle class do not feel that they are. This is the opposite of the situation before 1997. In the 1990s, many people who were objectively classified as the working class identified themselves as belonging to *chungsancheung*. One survey conducted in the 1990s, for example, found that 40 percent of manual working-class respondents identified themselves as *chungsancheung* (Hong 2005, 116).[8] So, if middle-class identity had been inflated or exaggerated in the earlier period, it has become deflated in the current period.

One survey study looked into this discrepancy closely. Using 2013 survey data, the Hyundai Research Institute compared the *chungsancheung* size estimated by the official definition of middle income (50–150% of median income) with respondents' self-identification (HRI 2013). Results indicated that among those who are classified as middle class by the objective definition, only 45 percent regarded themselves as belonging to the *chungsancheung*. The rest (55%) said they were in the low-income group. Another study, based on the 2013 survey by the Korean Sociological Association mentioned above, found that even among those who are considered to be the "core middle class," only 33 percent identified themselves as *chungsancheung*; among the lower-middle-class respondents, only 15 percent felt that they belonged to the *chungsancheung* (Yee 2014).

This is an interesting puzzle. Why do people whose income status qualifies them to be called *chungsancheung* not feel they are members of this class? The answer is rather simple. Most people hold a much higher standard than the official one (50–150% of median income) to be middle class. If so, what would be the standard that most people have in mind to become *chungsancheung*? This question was explored extensively in a recent survey conducted jointly by Maekyung and JobsKorea (Kim and Park 2019). The survey asked the respondents what they thought was the standard income for being *chungsancheung*. The category of income selected most frequently by the respondents was 5–6 million won per month (about US$4,500–5,400). Korea's median monthly income in 2018 was 2.3 million won (about US$2,100). This means that most people regarded a level of income twice as high as the national median income as necessary for joining the middle class. The survey also asked about property ownership as a qualification for middle-class membership. The respondents chose 30–40 *pyong* apartments (99–132m^2), with a market price of around 5 billion won (about US$454,500), as a qualification of *chungsancheung*. In addition to economic possession, the respondents also indicated that a certain "quality of life" is essential for belonging to the middle class. As an example, they felt that an ordinary middle-class family should be able to enjoy a dinner out about four times a month and be able to make one or two overseas leisure trips a year.

Thus, it is clear that the standard of living that most Koreans associate with *chungsancheung* has become much higher than it was in the past. This is a rather surprising finding considering the sluggish economic growth in recent decades. As sociologist Yee (2014, 129) observes, "Those who live in 30+ *pyong* housing, who earn more than 90 percent of the national average income, and who have received higher than community college–level education and work in semiprofessional or higher-status occupations must be those who lead a better than average life in Korea by the objective standard. Yet, the fact that many of them feel they are not *chungsancheung* means that the standard of *chungsancheung* has risen unrealistically high." Yee is absolutely right. But we must ask why this phenomenon has happened in Korea today.

The main reasons for this unrealistically high standard conjured up as a qualification of *chungsancheung* membership among Koreans, I believe, are the rise of the affluent segment of the middle class and the new consumption pattern and lifestyle that its members have developed as a strategy of separating themselves from average middle-class people. As we will see in the subsequent chapters, the adverse trend of income distribution in Korea since the late 1990s has produced a small minority of affluent families who are eager to establish their privileged status through conspicuous consumption and the upscale lifestyle. As the Korean economy has become globalized, Korea's consumption market has greatly expanded, and luxury consumption has become a dominant trend. The new rich can now enjoy all kinds of luxury goods and leisure opportunities that were unavailable in the past. And ordinary middle-class people try to imitate the consumption pattern and lifestyle of the well-to-do. Since most of the new rich used to be their peers, most middle-class people do not want to be left behind and try to catch up with them.

In the eyes of most middle-income people, the new standard of *chungsancheung* is what they observe in the lifestyle of the new rich. The emergence of Gangnam as a predominantly upper-middle–class town has facilitated such a perception. The media has also contributed greatly to the changing image of the middle class. Through TV dramas, commercial advertisements, and Internet materials, the media constantly highlight the lifestyles of the new rich, making it appear as if this is a new norm of respectability. Judged by that norm, unrealistically high as it may be, it is not surprising that many middle-income people feel they are no longer *chungsancheung*. In short, the meaning of *chungsancheung* has changed as a consequence of rising inequality, which has led to intensifying status competition in this era of hyperconsumerism.

2
RISING INEQUALITY

South Korea enjoyed moderate economic inequality despite the rapid pace of economic growth in the second half of the twentieth century.[1] Almost the entire population of the nation experienced steadily growing incomes and a remarkable improvement in their living standards. Even during the period of rapid industrial transformation in the 1970s and 1980s, income inequality remained at a modest level, at least compared with other countries. Thus, South Korea, along with the other Asian "little tigers" (Taiwan, Singapore, and Hong Kong), has been admired for having achieved what economists call "growth with equity" and "shared prosperity" (World Bank 1993). In recent years, however, the situation has almost completely reversed. Korea is no longer a society of moderate inequality; in fact, the level of income inequality is approaching that in the United States, which is the highest among the OECD economies.

During the past two decades, income distribution in Korea has shown a polarizing trend of two kinds: (1) polarization in the labor market according to employment status, producing large income differentials between regular (or standard) workers and nonregular (nonstandard) workers and between those employed at large firms and at small- to medium-sized firms, and (2) polarization between a minority of top income earners and the rest of the labor force (in the bottom 80 percent of the income hierarchy). This pattern of income distribution has led to internal division in both the working class and the middle class and to the blurring boundary between these two classes.

Income Distribution Trend

Korea's income distribution pattern since 1990 as measured by the Gini coefficient is presented in figure 2.1, which shows declining income inequality during the first half of the 1990s, a continuation of the favorable income distribution of the 1980s (the earlier data are not presented here due to inconsistent measures of inequality in the different periods). Previous studies have indicated that Korea experienced a substantial reduction of income inequality during the 1960s, with some increase during the 1970s, and then a long period of declining inequality from the early 1980s to the early 1990s (Kwak and Lee 2007; Kim 2012; Ryu 2012; Shin 2013; Cheon and Shin 2016). But income inequality began to increase from the mid-1990s, with the most dramatic increase during the Asian financial crisis

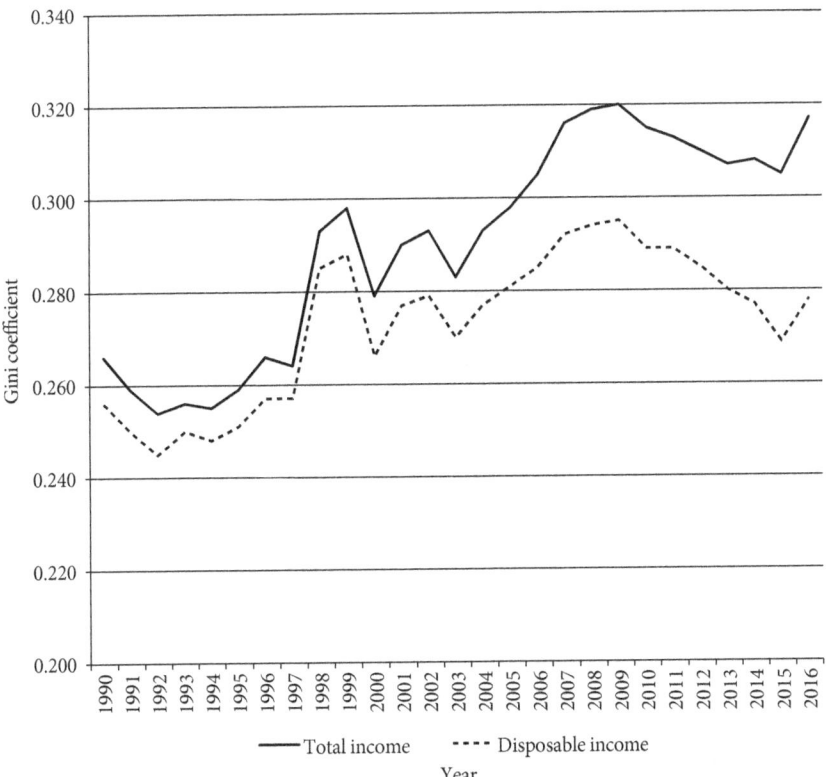

FIGURE 2.1. Trend in Gini coefficients (1990–2016)

Note: Income refers to household income divided by the number of household members (equivalized household income) based on national surveys of urban households with two or more household members.
Source: Korean Statistical Information Service, various years.

(1997–1999), increasing from 0.259 in 1995 to 0.298 in 1999. Income inequality dropped for two years but then continued to increase until it reached 0.320 in 2009. It began to decline again from 2009 but then began to increase again from 2016.

The acceleration of income inequality in the recent past is more evident if we examine the other popular measure of income inequality, the shares of decile income groups. The ratio of income share for the upper 10 percent compared to that of the bottom 10 percent changed from 3.30 in 1990 to 3.75 in 2000, to 4.90 in 2010, and to 5.01 in 2016.

Korea's Gini coefficient of 0.302 in 2013 (measured by household income distribution) was slightly lower than the OECD average of 0.316, with Korea ranking seventeenth of the thirty-four OECD member countries. But in terms of the Gini coefficient based on individual income, Korea shows one of the highest rates of inequality (Cheon and Shin 2016). This discrepancy is due to Korea having more income earners per household than other advanced economies. Korea's ratio of income for the top 10 percent compared to the bottom 10 percent was 4.78, very close to the 4.89 for the United States, which is the highest among the OECD countries. These data indicate that South Korea has experienced an accelerating trend of income inequality more abruptly than most other advanced economies in recent years.

A general consensus among analysts of Korean inequality is that the Asian financial crisis marked a turning point in Korea's income distribution trend (Kim 2012; Shin 2013; Joo 2015; Cheon 2016). The great economic setback during this period and the extensive neoliberal reform that followed are widely understood as major causes of the accelerating income inequality. But attributing the increasing inequality entirely to the financial crisis may be unwarranted. After all, as the data in figure 2.1 indicate, inequality began to increase from 1995, two years before the crisis. We must consider other broad structural factors to account for this change such as the Korean economy's transition to technology- and capital-intensive industries, economic liberalization, and Korea's increasing economic dependence on the Chinese market. Also important are major demographic shifts involving the rise of single families, a high divorce rate, and an aging population, (Shin and Kong 2014). All these changes have intensified since the 1990s and have affected Korea's income distribution in a significant way. Nonetheless, there seems to be no question that the financial crisis played a crucial role in changing Korea's income distribution. The sharpest rise of income inequality occurred in the four-year period during and after the crisis. The Gini coefficient of 0.266 in 1996 rose to 0.298 by 2000, increasing 12 percent in four years. The ratio of the top 10 percent compared to the bottom 10 percent increased from 3.46 to 4.16 during the same period, which clearly set the pattern for the continuous rise of inequality in the succeeding period.

What distinguishes the post-1990s period from the earlier period is not just a higher level of inequality but also its more complex pattern. In order to understand this change adequately, we need to examine two dimensions of growing inequality in the recent period: (1) inequality that has been boosted by sectoral divisions in the labor market between regular workers and irregular workers and between employees of large firms and those of smaller firms and (2) inequality that has occurred in the upper echelons of the income hierarchy, separating a minority of top income earners from the rest of the population. Most studies on Korean inequality tend to focus on either of these two processes, but here I want to give a more comprehensive picture of Korea's income distribution by considering both a horizontal labor market mechanism and a vertical mechanism of income divergence.

Labor Market Cleavages

One of the most important consequences of the Asian financial crisis was the revision of labor laws in 1998 that allowed firms to lay off redundant workers easily and replace regular workers with nonregular or nonstandard workers. Korean capitalists had attempted to change the labor laws in 1995 but met huge labor resistance and achieved only limited success. But thanks to the crisis environment and the strong pressure exercised by the Kim Dae Jung government (1998–2002), they were able to carry out a neoliberal reform through the Tripartite Committee (representing labor, business, and government). The immediate result of this labor law revision was a sharp rise in layoffs and the replacement of regularly hired workers with temporary or other contingent workers. Consequently, the number of nonstandard, nonregular workers increased dramatically during the immediate post–financial crisis period. According to government labor statistics, the proportion of irregular workers (including temporary workers and daily workers) increased from 41.9 percent in 1995 to 52.1 percent in 2000. But according to an independent labor research group, the ratio of irregular workers soared from 43.2 percent of all paid employees in 1996 to 58.4 percent in 2000. The government developed a standard definition of irregular workers in 2002 and began to measure its size with this new definiton. According to this definition, the category of irregular workers includes temporary workers, limited-term contract workers, subcontract workers, dispatch workers, independent-contract workers, home workers, and daily hires. This is the same category of

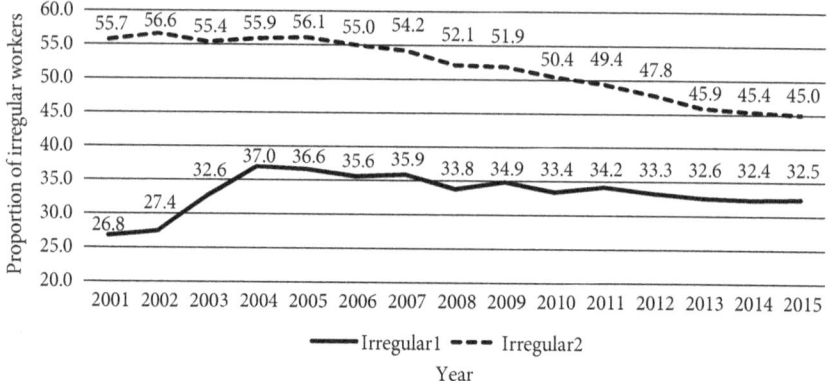

FIGURE 2.2. Proportion of irregular workers

Note: Irregular1 is based on the government definition of irregular workers, and Irregular2 is based on labor advocacy groups' definitions.
Source: Korea Labor Institute and Korea Labor and Society Institute, various years.

workers often referred to as nonstandard or precarious workers in other countries. Regular workers, on the other hand, include the full-time employed with a long-term employment contract. According to government statistics, the proportion of irregular workers increased sharply from 26.8 percent in 2001 to 37.0 percent in 2004 and then began to decrease gradually, at an exceedingly slow pace, to 33.8 percent in 2008 and to 32.5 percent in 2015 (see figure 2.2). The important fact here is that even in the mid-2010s, about 33 percent (by government statistics) to 45 percent (labor groups' statistics) of the Korean workforce was employed in nonregular, precarious jobs. And they were found in every industry and every type and size of firms; even the public sector held about 20 percent of its employees in irregular positions in the 2010s (A. Kim 2004; Shin 2012; Kim 2015; Lee 2015).

Regular versus Irregular Workers

The rise of irregular workers since the early 1990s and the stubborn continuation of their large presence, despite several policy measures adopted to reduce this number, tell much about the precarious condition of the labor market for Korea's working population. These trends also reveal a new major source of growing inequality in Korean society. As shown in table 2.1, the average income of irregular workers in 2010 was 54.8 percent of that of regular workers (based on government statistics). The differential remained about the same in 2015, at 54.4 percent. On average, irregular workers earned about half of regular work-

TABLE 2.1 Ratio of irregular workers' wages to regular workers' wages

WAGE	2002	2005	2010	2015
Regular workers	100	100	100	100
Irregular workers 1	67.1	62.7	54.8	54.4
Irregular workers 2	52.7	50.9	46.9	49.8

Note: Irregular workers 1 is based on the government definition of irregular workers, and irregular workers 2 is based on labor advocacy groups' definitions.

Source: KLI (Korea Labor Institute), KLSI (Korea Labour and Society Institute), various years.

ers' wages for the same number of hours worked. This is a relatively new phenomenon of twenty-first-century Korea, as this labor market duality did not play such an important role in producing income differentials in the pre-1990 period. Korea had many temporary and daily workers even before the Asian financial crisis. But during that time, regular and irregular workers did not really constitute two sharply distinguished categories of laborers. This was because the job market was more open and fluid and allowed easy mobility from temporary to permanent job positions. In addition, even the regular workers with standard contracts were not well protected by labor laws, unions, or the government. Since the late 1990s, however, firms have deliberately attempted to use nonstandard workers as a chief means of reducing labor costs and counterbalancing the legally protected regular workers.

Today, irregular workers are also greatly disadvantaged in terms of other forms of compensation and social protection. Most of them receive no severance pay, medical insurance, or other company welfare subsidies that are available to regular workers. Irregular workers are also barred from joining the unions that represent regular workers. There do exist a very few unions specifically organized to represent irregular workers, but they represent less than 2 percent of irregular workers and are largely powerless to improve their second-class status in the labor market. (In 2015, 1.9 percent of irregular workers and 20.9 percent of regular workers belonged to unions.) What makes it worse is that opportunities to move from nonregular to regular jobs are very limited in the Korean labor market. According to one study made in the 2010s, 22.4 percent of irregular workers moved to regular job status after three years of employment, while 50.9 percent continued to work as irregular laborers and 26.7 percent became unemployed (OECD 2015).

The population groups most likely to be found in nonregular jobs are young people (under twenty years old) and older people (over sixty years old). They are also more likely to be women than men. In 2015, almost 90 percent of workers under age twenty were employed in irregular jobs. Many of them were college

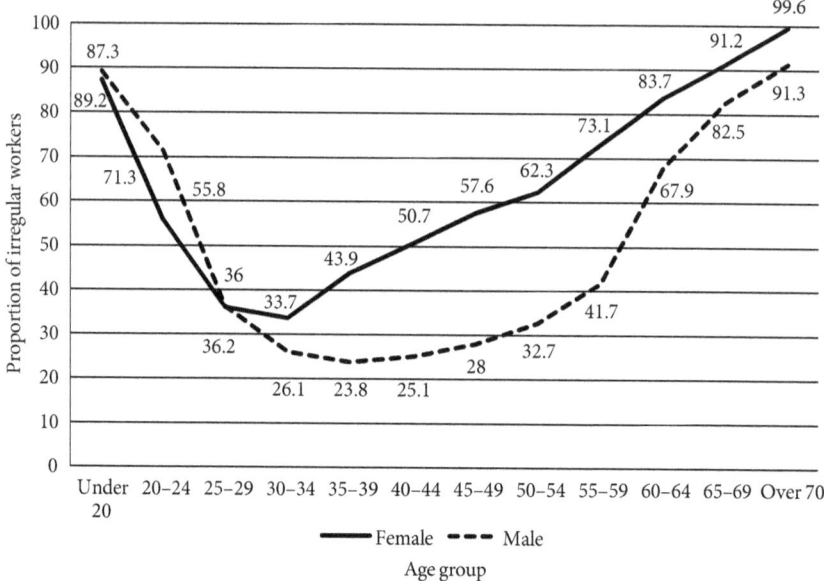

FIGURE 2.3. Proportion of irregular workers by age and gender
Source: KLSI (2012, 2015).

students working as part-time hires earning minimum hourly wages in the service sector. The proportion of irregular workers also increased sharply in the age groups above age sixty (see figure 2.3).

Gender plays an equally important role in determining employment status. In 2015, 55.3 percent of employed women held irregular jobs, compared to 36.4 percent of irregularly employed men. Among those aged thirty to thirty-four, 36.7 percent of women workers were in irregular jobs, while 25.1 percent of the men were irregular workers. And for those aged thirty-five to thirty-nine, 45.0 percent of women and 23.5 percent of men who were employed held irregular jobs. While the probability of being pushed into irregular jobs increases greatly when male workers enter their fifties, for female workers this occurs when they are in their early thirties.

Large versus Smaller Firms

Another important sectoral cleavage that has developed during the past two decades is between large firms and smaller firms. Since the financial crisis, a small number of Korea's large firms have adapted to global challenges successfully, while most medium- to small-sized firms have barely survived the increasing international competition from emerging economies. This unbalanced growth of Korean industry has resulted in widening inequality between different types of firms in recent decades. In the pre-1990s period, pay differences between large and medium to small-sized firms were relatively modest but increased significantly afterward. Table 2.2 shows that the average income at medium to small-sized firms was as large as 96.7 percent of the average income at large firms (three hundred or more employees) in 1980. But this ratio (wage level at smaller firms compared to that of large firms) decreased to 79.9 percent in 1990, 71.3 percent in 2000, and then 62.9 in 2010. Fortunately, the gap remained at that level in 2014. But an important fact is that the income differential between employees of large and smaller firms is almost as large as that between regular and irregular workers. In fact, a well-known Korean labor market analyst, Jung (2013), argues that income disparity between large and smaller firms is a more serious problem in Korea today than that between regular and irregular workers. This large income differential between large and smaller firms is due to many factors, but a critical reason is that many smaller firms have become subcontractors to large firms and are subjected to highly unfair and exploitative business relationship with the latter. More troubling is that the Korean industrial structure has become more severely unbalanced and dualistic in the global era, with only a small proportion of the nation's labor force employed at large firms, while the majority work at medium- and small-sized firms. In 2014, 81 percent of the total labor force was employed at medium- to small-sized firms, while only 19 percent was employed at large firms.

But all large firms are not the same. A great difference in wage levels exists between conglomerate (chaebol) firms and the rest of the large firms. For example, in 2014 while the average annual income for the employees of large firms (employing three hundred or more) was about US$52,000, the pay of employees of Samsung Electronic was about US$92,000, and that of Hyundai Motors employees was about US$88,000. This means that the average income at most large firms was less than 60 percent of income at top chaebol firms (Chang 2015).

TABLE 2.2 Income differentials between large and smaller firms

	1980	1990	2000	2010	2014
Large firms	100	100	100	100	100
Smaller firms	96.7	79.9	71.3	62.9	62.3

Note: Large firms = 300 or more employees; smaller firms = less than 300 employees.

Source: Chang 2015, 94.

In short, two prominent factors have emerged as critical causal factors of income determination in addition to educational and other demographic factors: employment status (regular vs. irregular) and the size of the enterprise where one is employed. Although these two factors were not unimportant before the 1990s, their wage-differentiating effects have become far greater in the twenty-first century. The aggressive neoliberal globalization that the South Korean economy has pursued over the past two decades has increased the causal power of these two job market factors, thereby increasing the level of income inequality in Korea.

Self-Employment Sector

Along with these adverse changes occurring in the job market for the employed labor force, a no less grim reality exists in the world of self-employment. Korea has traditionally had a large number of self-employed workers. In 2014 the self-employed accounted for 27 percent of the Korean labor force, which was the fourth-highest rate among the thirty-four OECD countries. The absolute majority of them (about 74 percent) are solo operators with no employees. Their businesses are heavily concentrated in retail and restaurant industries and in some personal services.

In the past, small independent businesses provided job opportunities to many new urban migrants from the countryside. Many small business owners who lacked adequate formal education were still able to earn a decent income and accumulate a modest amount of assets, thereby becoming able to climb up to the middle class. They purchased houses of their own, sent their children to college, and were able to maintain a decent middle-class lifestyle. Thus, independent businesses functioned as an alternative channel for upward social mobility in the rapidly industrializing Korean society.

But the world of small business has experienced much adverse change in the 2000s. First, the independent business sector became saturated with many new entrants who had been pushed out of their formal employment. Many white-collar and managerial workers who had been laid off found no other alternatives in the labor market and decided to start a new business, often with hardly any business experience. While the number of small businesses continued to increase, the slowdown of the economy depressed consumption demands. Even worse, large conglomerate firms were encroaching into small business sectors at the same time. Eating and drinking places, supermarkets, and service businesses have been increasingly taken over by chain stores run by chaebol-level firms.

In such a business environment, the failure rate is bound to be very high and the income situation of the self-employed very poor. According to national statistics, more than half of newly started small businesses go bankrupt within three years (Lee 2015). The economic situation of the self-employed can be seen by comparing their income with those of wage-earning workers. The average monthly income of the self-employed in 2014 was about 60 percent of the monthly income of regularly employed workers. This is a remarkable drop from the past when the average earnings of the self-employed were about the same as the income of the average wage worker. In 1990 the average income among the self-employed was 95 percent of the average wage income, but this dropped to 88 percent in 2000 and continued to decline to 60 percent in 2014. Thus, as Lee (2015, 189) argues, "it is crucial to approach the self-employed in Korea as an insecure class" because "the lower strata of this sector suffer from excessive competition, low levels of net profit, a high burden of household debt, extended working hours, and few possibilities for social advancement." Thus, the job market position of many self-employed workers is as precarious as that of nonregular workers (though they constitute two separate categories in labor statistics).

Income Concentration at the Top

Along with growing inequality based on employment status, another important trend to notice in Korea is the increasing concentration of income at the top of the income hierarchy. That is the form of inequality on which this book primarily focuses. Reliable studies on income concentration among the rich in Korea were sparse until recently. But given the gravity of inequality issues in Korea today and thanks to the influence of Piketty's (2014) landmark study of income inequality in advanced capitalism, Korean scholars have begun to produce reliable analyses of income concentration at the top (Kim 2012; Hong 2015; Joo 2015). They have followed a similar methodology to that of Piketty, relying more on tax data than household survey data, which are known to underrepresent income earners at both the top and the bottom. Among others, Nak Nyeon Kim and his colleagues have done intensive analyses of Korea's top income distribution in recent years; I rely heavily on their studies in this chapter (Kim 2012; Kim and Kim 2015; N. Kim 2016).

Figure 2.4 presents data on the changing shares of national income received by upper-income groups (top 1 percent, 5 percent, and 10 percent) over the past three decades. The data used for this analysis are from the World Top Income Database (2015), the original sources of which are tax reports compiled by each nation's tax bureau. Data displayed in figure 2.4 show that compared to the earlier

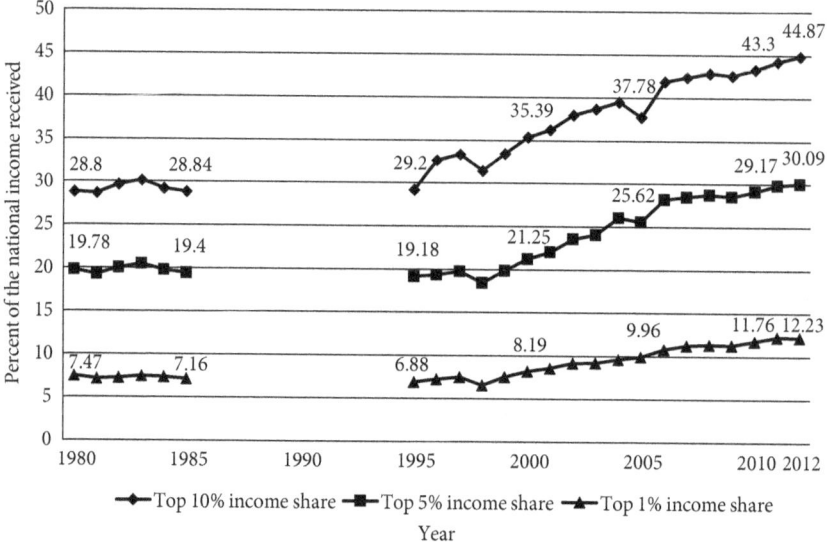

FIGURE 2.4. Ratio of income share by top income groups

Source: World Income Database (reproduced from Chang 2015).

period (1980–1985) when the shares of top income groups hardly changed, the post-1990s period saw significant income growth among those belonging to the upper 10 percent of the income hierarchy. The income share of the upper 10 percent, for example, had remained constant at 28 percent from 1980 to 1985 but began to increase drastically from 29.2 percent in 1995 to 44.8 percent in 2012. Similarly, income shares of the top 5 percent and top 1 percent did not increase but actually decreased slightly between 1980 and 1985, but in the recent period they increased dramatically. The top 5 percent income share increased from 19.2 percent to 30.1 percent between 1995 and 2012, while that of the top 1 percent increased from 6.9 percent to 12.2 percent. The data clearly demonstrate that the post-1990s neoliberal era was a period of rapid income concentration in the top income groups.[2]

In their more detailed analysis, Kim and Kim (2015, 16) confirmed that income concentration has been more dramatic at the very top of the income pyramid: "While the top 1 percent wage income share increased from 4.89 percent in 1995 to 7.45 percent in 2010, the top 0.1 percent wage income share increased faster from 1.27 percent to 2.16 percent during the same period. It implies that the average wage of the top 0.1 percent wage earners in 2010 was 21.6 times greater than the average wage of all wage earners whereas it was just 12.7 times greater in 1995."

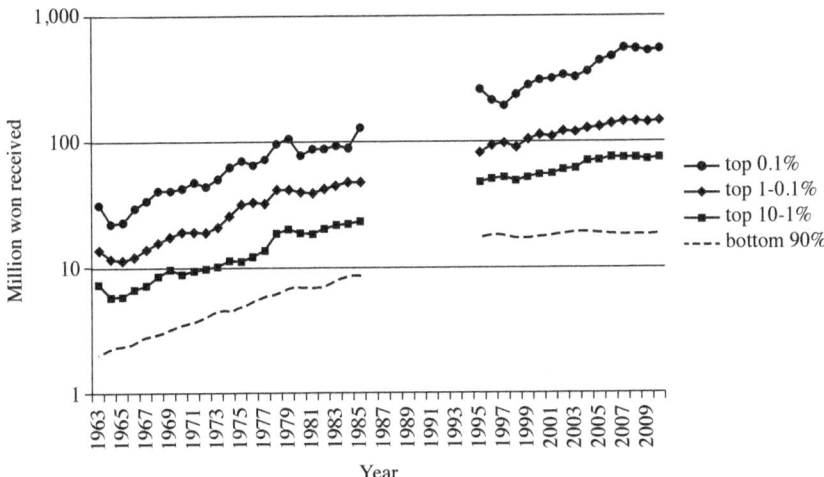

FIGURE 2.5. Average wage income by income groups in Korea, 1993–2009 (Unit: 1 million *won*)

Note: The wage income is adjusted according to constant 2010 prices in log scale.
Source: Kim and Kim (2015).

This changing pattern of income distribution in favor of the upper-income groups can be seen more concretely by examining the actual amounts of income received by different income groups over the longer period of Korean development. The data presented in figure 2.5 display the change in average income (expressed in Korean *won*) received by different decile income groups from 1995 to 2010. This figure again demonstrates that during the earlier period of rapid industrialization, all income groups saw their income grow at a similar rate. Remarkably, the bottom 90 percent experienced the same rate of wage growth as that of the top 10 percent. Since the Asian financial crisis, however, we see a markedly different pattern. Wage increase for the average workers has been minimal, while income for the upper 10 percent has continued to increase. What is more, of the top 10 percent, income for the top 0.1 percent increased much faster.

We can consider several factors that have contributed to income concentration at the top: structural, technical, and policy-related. In terms of structural factors, the most important is that by the 1990s the South Korean economy had become a technology- and knowledge-intensive economy and began to transfer low-skilled manufacturing production to low-wage economies such as China, Vietnam, and Indonesia. This industrial transition has naturally increased the value of high technical skills. Those who possessed scarce professional and technical skills came to command exceptionally high remuneration. Since the 1990s, Korea's large firms have gradually replaced their old seniority-based payment system with a performance-based system. Thus, intrafirm pay differentials widened as pay became tied to employees' skill levels and job performances, contributing to the overall increase of income inequality.

Furthermore, a significant change has occurred in the governance system in large conglomerate firms since the 1990s. Most conglomerate firms began to adopt the Anglo-Saxon corporate governance system that is oriented to the interests of stock owners, equity financing, and short-term performance in the stock market. This transition has also been accelerated by a growing number of foreign shareholders that began to influence the governance systems in large Korean firms (Chung et. al 2008; Kim and Kim 2015). With this corporate change, the CEOs began to play a far more important role than before and command exceptionally high salaries and other financial rewards. So, as in other advanced economies, the neoliberal transition of the Korean economy has produced what Piketty (2014) calls the "supermanager" or "super salariat" phenomenon, in which top CEOs receive tremendously high salaries plus lucrative packages of financial compensation.[3]

If the newly emerging group of CEOs constitutes a major part of the super-rich in Korea today, another important group is composed of high-income professionals. One study of the occupational composition of the upper 1 percent found that the majority are professional and managerial workers in the medical and financial sectors (Hong 2015). Particularly important occupational groups are medical doctors, pharmacists, and financial specialists. Most likely, they are the ones who possess special skills and reputations in their fields and may also own independent businesses. The rise of financial specialists among the top income group must be closely related to the financialization of the Korean economy, an essential feature of neoliberalization in all advanced economies (Harvey 2005; Kotz 2015; Steger and Roy 2021).

Outside the occupational system, another factor that facilitated income concentration at the top in Korea was a change in the tax system, more specifically the reduction of tax rates for the rich. The highest statutory marginal tax rates for the top 0.1 percent income level were as high as 70 percent in the second half of the 1970s but decreased to 50 percent in the first half of the 1990s and then further to about 35 percent in the 2000s (Kim and Kim 2015). During this period, capital income increased much faster than wage income among top income earners. Thus, the combined effect of these two factors must have contributed greatly to the rapid wealth accumulation at the top.

We have considered only income inequality so far. Comparatively, data on wealth inequality are sparse. But thanks to growing scholarly interest in the economic concentration at the top, more reliable data on household assets have

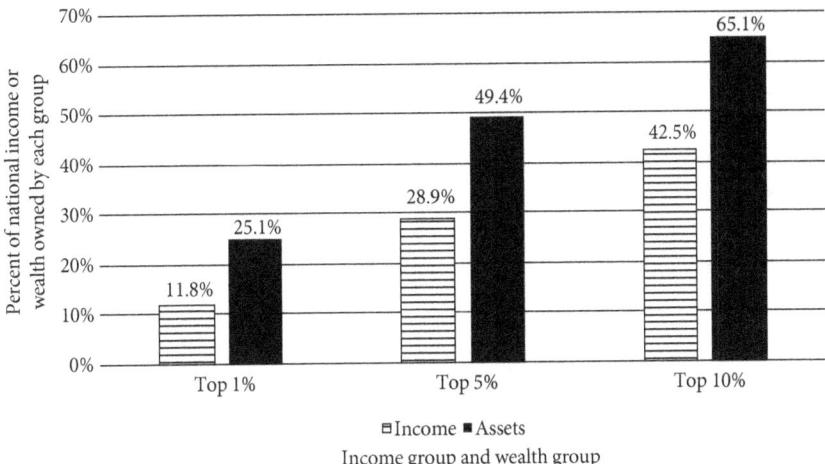

FIGURE 2.6. Income and asset shares by top income groups, 2011–2013

Source: N. Kim (2016, 2018).

recently become available. The general pattern is that wealth inequality is much larger than income inequality in Korea, which is consistent with the findings in most other societies. Figure 2.6 presents data on wealth distribution based on inheritance tax information and compares the proportions of national wealth possessed by the top economic groups with their income shares (N. Kim 2016, 2018). During 2011–2013, the top 1 percent received 25.1 percent of the national wealth, while the top 10 percent received 65.1 percent. In the same period, the top 1 percent income group received 11.8 percent of the national income, while the upper 10 percent received 42.5 percent. We can see that wealth inequality is about two times larger than income inequality and becomes larger as we go up the distribution ladder. This is because the rich are distinguished from the rest by their financial ownership more than by earned income.

Forms of Polarization

The data we have examined thus far have confirmed a powerful trend of polarization occurring in Korean society in the neoliberal era. This polarization is not a simple process of dividing the population into two classes of rich and poor or capital and labor. Therefore, we need to consider this process more carefully. Basically, what we have observed are two forms of polarization. One is the widening gap between the top income group and the rest of the population, with a heavy concentration of income at the top and declining income in the middle.

The other is growing income disparity occurring in the labor market between regular and nonregular workers and between employees of large firms and medium- and small-sized firms.

The first form of economic polarization is a well-known phenomenon in most advanced industrial societies. The Occupy Wall Street movement in the United States that occurred in the aftermath of the 2007–2008 global financial crisis popularized the phrase "the top 1 percent versus the bottom 99 percent," and this idea has resonated with many other societies. Piketty's (2014) influential book has provided compelling evidence of income polarization in all advanced capitalist economies, and Stiglitz (2011, 2012) has provided a powerful analysis of its manifestation in the United States, while Milanovic (2016) has also provided rich information on the global inequality pattern. The data reviewed above confirm that Korea is not an exception. In fact, South Korea has experienced this polarization process more intensely than most other industrial societies in recent decades. Thus, the image of a polarized society divided between the top 1 percent and the bottom 99 percent eminently applies to today's Korean society.

But if we look at the income distribution pattern more closely, it is not just the upper 1 percent but rather a broader segment, including the top 10 percent, who have experienced a substantial increase in their income share during the past two decades. The data in figure 2.4 reveal that the average income level among the upper 10 percent group has grown almost as fast as that of the upper 1 percent, in contrast to the stagnating income among the bottom 90 percent. Most likely, those in the upper 10 percent income bracket are higher-level professional, managerial, and technical workers whose income has grown rapidly during the decades of the neoliberal transition in the Korean economy. They are the elite workers employed in the leading sectors of the economy and have benefited from the globalization of the economic system. The upper 10 percent group also includes nonsalaried wealthy people who have accumulated wealth through real estate investment during the housing market bubbles of the past two or three decades. In fact, many professional and managerial people have also become well-to-do through investing in the real estate market.

Thus, we can look at the economic polarization in Korea as involving two tiers. At the first tier we have the division between the top 1 percent and the bottom 99 percent, while at the second tier we have the division between the upper 10 percent and the bottom 90 percent. These are not separate phenomena. If the top 1 percent represents the large capitalists, the upper 10 percent includes top managers and professionals who serve the capitalist class. The wealth differential between the two groups is very large, but they share a common interest in and are benefited by the same capitalist system. Both groups have benefited greatly from Korea's shift to an advanced and globalized economy and have emerged as the real winners of the neoliberal transition.

The second form of polarization has occurred within the larger working class, along the axes of labor market segmentation discussed above, between regular and nonregular workers and between employees of large firms and those of medium- and small-sized firms. Presumably, this labor market polarization has a more divisive impact on the rank-and-file workers than among the upper 10 percent or 20 percent. These two axes of labor market division cut across industrial and occupational categories, producing internal divisions within the working class and the middle class while blurring the boundary between these two classes. Thus, the class situation of white-collar workers employed on nonstandard contracts or at small-sized firms would occupy an inferior position to that of regular blue-collar workers employed at large conglomerate firms. In the new labor market, occupational category is less significant in one's class position; instead, labor market position, defined by level of job security and the social protection attached to it, has become critical in determining class.

As described earlier, the Korean working class had been relatively homogeneous during the period of rapid industrialization, with no sharp divisions based on types of employment or the size of firms where individuals are employed. But much change has occurred in this regard. In many large firms today, regular and irregular workers constitute almost two different working classes. Similarly, blue-collar workers at large firms and at smaller firms are located in significantly different market positions in terms of income and social protection, regardless of their status as regular or irregular workers. While all the workers at smaller firms suffer low wages, the blue-collar workers at large conglomerate firms have seen their wages increase tremendously since the 1990s, especially if they are members of powerful unions. Defined frequently as a "labor aristocracy" by the media and conservative politicians, these privileged workers now belong to the middle class in terms of their economic and social status. Thus, the working class has lost much of the internal class homogeneity that existed during the early period of rapid industrialization led by the authoritarian developmental state.

Middle-Class Decline and Internal Division

More interesting and complex changes have occurred in the Korean middle class. Having seen the vigorous growth of the middle class in the industrial era, Korea has experienced a significant decline of this class since the Asian financial crisis.

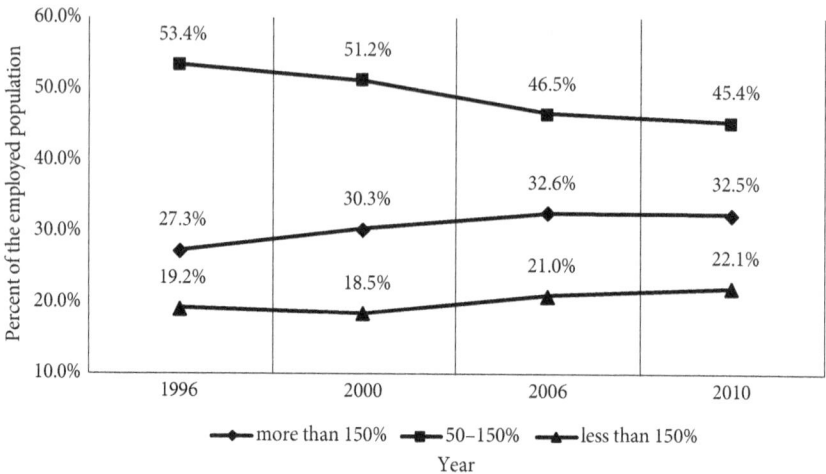

FIGURE 2.7. Relative size of three income groups, 1996–2010

Note: Income groups are determined by each group's income position relative to the median income of the nation. Income data were drawn from national household surveys plus individual tax reports.
Source: Adapted from Kim (2012, 23).

The data presented in figures 2.7 and 2.8 show the changing lot of three income classes: those earning more than 150 percent of the median income, those earning 50–150 percent, and those earning 50 percent or less.[4] Figure 2.7 shows that while the upper- and lower-income groups increased in size, the middle-income group (50–150%) shrank. Between 1996 and 2010, the proportion of the upper-income group increased from 27.3 percent to 32.5 percent of the labor force, and the lower group also grew from 19.2 percent to 22.1 percent. In sharp contrast, the middle-income group declined from 53.4 percent to 45.4 percent. Thus, the shrinking middle class in Korea is as serious a social problem as in most other advanced industrial societies.

Figure 2.8 presents the share of national income distributed to each income class between 1996 and 2010. The data demonstrate that the income share for the upper-income group increased from 51.0 percent to 65.5 percent, while the share for the bottom-income group decreased slightly from 5.1 percent to 4.3 percent. In contrast, the income share for the middle-income group decreased from 43.9 percent to 30.2 percent. Clearly, the shifts in income distribution during the past decade and a half have been most favorable to the upper third (more accurately, the top echelons of this statistical group) and most unfavorable to the middle-income earners. Significantly, it is the middle-income group rather than the low-income group that has experienced the most negative consequences of neoliberal globalization during this period.

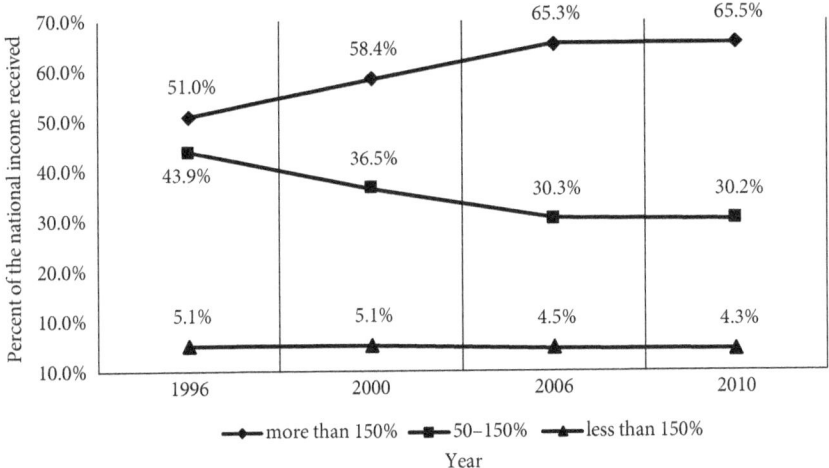

FIGURE 2.8. Income share of three income groups, 1996–2010

Note: Income groups are determined by each group's income position relative to the median income of the nation. Income data were drawn from national household surveys plus individual tax reports.
Source: Adapted from Kim (2012, 23).

But we should be wary of interpreting these data to mean that the whole middle class has suffered an economic decline. The operational definition of the middle-income class as those earning 50–150 percent of the median income was introduced by the OECD and is widely used in many international studies, including those on Korea. But the problem with this measure is that it classifies many people who are normally regarded as the upper segment of the middle class into the upper-income class. In Korea as in other advanced economies, most of those who are earning more than 150 percent of the median income are likely to be professional and managerial workers or small- and medium-sized business owners. Sociologically speaking, they represent the upper middle class rather than the upper class. By excluding many high-income groups from the middle-class category, most statistical approaches to the middle class miss the opportunity to examine an important change occurring in that middle space.[5]

As we can see, the upper 10 percent income group has experienced substantial income growth in the past two decades. In fact, other studies suggest that the upper 20 percent of income groups has also increased their share of income in the past two decades (Kim 2012; Kim and Kim 2015; Cheon 2016). Where to draw a meaningful boundary between the upper middle and the rest of the middle is a tricky question. Some argue that a truly significant class boundary exists at the upper 5 percent, separating what could be called the meritocratic elite from the ordinary middle class. But it is more common among analysts to distinguish the upper 10 percent from the bottom 90 percent. Those who are in the income bracket of the top 1–10 percent are most likely to belong to the sociological category of the upper middle class.

In short, while it is true that the larger middle class has been declining and shrinking in the neoliberal era, not all of its members have suffered from the recent economic changes. Instead, the minority of its members (including high-earning professional and managerial workers and some small entrepreneurs) have actually benefited from the skewed income distribution and has emerged as the new affluent middle class. The consequence is the internal division between this new affluent middle class and the ordinary middle class. Further, this division is becoming more important in determining individuals' life chances and lifestyles than the traditional boundary between the working class and the middle class.

3

CONSUMPTION AND CLASS DISTINCTION

Consumption plays a critical role in determining social status in all modern societies. In Korea, the concept of *chungsancheung* (middle class) is primarily defined in terms of consumption status. Maintaining a certain respectable level of consumption has always been regarded as an essential requirement for middle-class status in South Korea (Lett 1998; Yang 1999; Hart 2001). But during the early days of Korea's economic development, consumption played a relatively minor role in class distinction. The main reason was, of course, the underdeveloped domestic market due to the lower living standards of Korean people at that time. But an equally important reason was the tight control that the Park Chung Hee government maintained on imports of consumer goods and a strong antipathy of the political leadership against conspicuous consumption by the rich (Nelson 2000). However, the consumption world started to change noticeably when the South Korean economy began to be liberalized in the 1980s. In addition to continuous economic growth, democratization in 1987 and the Olympic Games in 1988 facilitated a liberal social atmosphere and rising consumerism in Korea. Then the 1997–1998 Asian financial crisis forced Korea to open its markets widely and accept an increasing volume of imports and foreign direct investments. The shock of the financial crisis helped to remove not only government sanctions on imports but also public resistance to luxury consumption among the rich by establishing neoliberalism as a hegemonic ideology. This change, of course, did not occur overnight, but the public slowly began to accept the fact that the rich are entitled to spend their money any way they want. The state, which had once preached against overspending (*kwasobi*), began to tell people that for the Korean economy to continue to export, the Korean people must be willing to reciprocate by consuming more imports from the trading economies.

A Craze for Luxury (*Myongpoom*)

The most noticeable change in Korea's consumption market since the 1990s was the rise of luxury consumption. A new word that expresses this trend most clearly is *myongpoom*, which refers to prestigious or distinguished goods. Introduced by the marketing industry, the term has been part of the popular vocabulary in Korea since the mid-1990s. *Myongpoom* evokes fine art and craftsmanship of exceptional quality in contrast to ordinary products. But in actuality the term refers to luxury brand-name products imported mostly from Europe. The *myongpoom* label is attached to any expensive brand-name product, including accessories, handbags, clothes, jewelry, fragrances, cosmetics, and other personal items, all carrying well-known logos such as Louis Vuitton, Gucci, Chanel, Prada, and Hermes. Most of these items are for women, but a few, such as luxury watches, European cars, and expensive golf sets, are favorite *myongpoom* for men.

The *myongpoom* market grew fast in the 1990s. Late in the decade, fashionable department stores in Seoul began to open *myongpoom* corners or even separate stores specializing in luxury brands. The first *myongpoom* department store, the Galeria (owned by the Hyundai conglomerate), opened in the wealthy Apgujeong neighborhood in Gangnam. This was followed by other *myongpoom* department stores established by other conglomerate firms such as the Samsung and Lotte groups. These luxury stores have prospered ever since, unaffected by the ups and downs of market conditions.

The main target of the *myongpoom* market is the new rich. The marketing industry has subtly promoted an image of *myongpoom* customers as a class of people who appreciate and can afford to possess fine-quality items—those who can discriminate the excellent from the ordinary and are therefore entitled to a certain degree of recognition and respect. Thus, *myongpoom* goods offer a status marker for people who have become rich and want to distinguish themselves from ordinary middle-class folks. Through exclusive consumption linked to the image of global bourgeois culture, the affluent segment of the Korean middle class has sought to establish a new class identity.

Although it started with the new rich, luxury consumption spread quickly to the larger middle class, especially those in their twenties and thirties. Unable to buy genuine *myongpoom* products, many of them turned to counterfeit *myongpoom*. These counterfeits are internally graded according to how closely they imitate the genuine products. Korea became well known for producing high-grade counterfeit brand products, most of which are now produced in and imported from China. Among the most popular *myongpoom* are Louis Vuitton handbags, genuine or fake. It was once said that about half of the women living in Seoul possessed such a bag. Counterfeits of *myongpoom* handbags and shoes were so widely available that a new status competition became focused on discerning the fake from the genuine. *Myongpoom* goods are used as special gifts among dating partners and have become almost mandatory items in wedding gift exchanges among middle-class families.

The luxury consumption trend is, of course, not limited to Korea. According to Chadha and Husband (2006), Asia's craze for brand-name products first took off in Japan and spread to the four little tiger economies, and now China is a hotbed of extravagant luxury consumption by the new rich. Asia consumes more than half of the world's brand-name products, and its new rich serve as a main target for global luxury industries. In their book *The Cult of the Luxury Brand*, Chadha and Husband (2006, 1) observe that "the cult of the luxury brand . . . is sweeping Asia, a phenomenon so powerful that the continent is now the biggest market in the world for Western luxury brands." They estimate that the Asian luxury goods market constitutes 37 percent of the global market of US$80 billion but is actually much higher if we include Asian tourists' shopping abroad. The main reason for the rise of luxury consumption seems more or less the same in all developing economies. These societies have undergone tremendous economic and social transitions within a few decades, spurring a shift away from status systems based on birth and traditional hierarchies and toward new systems in which status is determined by personal wealth and lifestyle; the best way to demonstrate this kind of status is through consumption (Chua 2000). In particular, the newly emerged rich want to establish their new class identity above the ordinary middle-class crowd through consuming luxurious products and adopting fashionable lifestyles borrowed from the middle-class culture of the advanced economies. As Chadha and Husband (2006, 2–3) argue, "In today's Asia you are what you *wear*. Those Gucci bags and Ferragamo shoes aren't merely girlish indulgences—neither are the Armani suits and Rolex watches just male vanity at work—they are part of a new social protocol where your identity and self-worth are determined by the visible brands on your body. . . . Luxury brands are a modern set of symbols that Asians are wearing to redefine their identity and social position" (2–3).

But to adequately understand today's luxury craze in Asia, we must look at not just the demand side of this consumption pattern—that is, the desire for status among Asia's new rich—but also the supply side of the consumption market, which is the way luxury goods are produced and marketed in the era of globalization. Until the early twentieth century, Europe's luxury goods truly represented the finest craftsmanship, with products created in small numbers by individual craftsmen catering exclusively to a select group of the upper class. But this changed in the last decades of the twentieth century. According to Dana Thomas (2008), the author of *Deluxe: How Luxury Lost Its Luster*, this change began to occur when a smart entrepreneur, Bernard Arnault, came up with the idea of using the mystique of the great brand names for mass marketing. Arnault started to buy up brands such as Dior and Vuitton, building them into large conglomerate structures. His key strategy was to put luxury-brand logos on mass-produced products (which Chadha and Husband call "logo-fication") and employ media-oriented advertising techniques. According to Chadha and Husband (2006, 20), "the logo-fication of bags was the single most important factor in spreading the luxury brand in Asia."

Reappropriation of the Traditional

An interesting change that has occurred in this new phase of class distinction is that the affluent began to turn to Korea's traditional cultural products as another means of confirming and demonstrating their status. The rich began to acquire old upper-class possessions, such as antique furniture, paintings, calligraphic works, pottery, china, and traditional costumes. Old *yangban* (aristocratic) culture was harnessed by the new rich as a source of possessions that could enhance their status by distinguishing them from others. This trend in turn encouraged Korean artisans to produce exclusive products for their rich clientele. Thus, the prices of artisan-made pottery, furniture, and art products have increased tremendously; some Korean artisan-made handbags are sold at prices equivalent to those of luxury brand-name imports. Moreover, traditional Korean housing materials and designs, such as yellow-mud and hot-floored (*ondol*) rooms, have become popular again, and traditional Korean-style houses (*hanok*), which had almost disappeared in the Korean housing market, became fashionable objects to own.

Along with this revival of traditional *yangban* arts and crafts has come a revival of traditional forms of family ceremonies. For instance, many newly emerged wealthy families invest substantially in the landscaping of their ancestral graveyards. This is an act of filial piety, the most important moral virtue in Confucian philosophy, but also a subtle status-enhancing strategy to demonstrate the family's respectability. A large beautifully landscaped graveyard on a clan-owned countryside hill serves as a powerful display of one's *yangban* lineage.

Another example is the revival of traditional wedding ceremonies. Weddings in most societies offer an arena par excellence for status competition. As Korea has become a modernized society, many people have abandoned the traditional wedding in favor of the Western-style wedding, conducted primarily at commercial wedding halls (Kendall 1996). Recently, however, a growing number of couples and their families have chosen to perform a traditional Confucian-style wedding in addition to the usual wedding hall ceremony. This used to be done among fashionable people in artistic circles but has now become the practice of an increasing number of well-to-do families. Unlike in the old days, the modern-day traditional wedding is a very costly event. Typically, it involves extravagant gift exchanges, special facilities in which to perform the extra wedding, an elegant banquet for the guests, elaborate professional photographing, and the like. Such a wedding is an expensive venture both economically and emotionally. For that precise reason, a traditional wedding serves as a means to demonstrate a family's comfortable economic status and its implicit title to *yangban* lineage.

Well-being Culture

Another distinct pattern of consumption that appeared as South Korea's economy reached a more mature stage of development is an increasing obsession (especially among the relatively well-to-do) with health and physical appearance and the willingness to spend money and time to achieve them. A new marketing label that appeared in the early 2000s and became widely used in the media and advertising was *welbing* (well-being). Well-being, of course, implies a healthier and wholesome quality of life. As *welbing* became popularized in Korea, however, it refers mainly to maintaining a good life through eating organically grown foods, drinking purified water, using supposedly healthful materials in the home, joining health clubs, practicing yoga, spending family weekends on a country farm, and the like. The commercial culture of well-being was quickly established around 2003, when a series of environmental crises, including the SARS epidemic, several waves of large-scale yellow dust storms originating in China and Mongolia, and shocking media revelations of contaminated food being sold, raised serious health concerns among Koreans. Suddenly Korean people, especially the wealthy, were willing to spend a lot of money to ensure better health for their families.

The well-being culture that spread quickly in the early 2000s commodified traditional notions of health and wholesomeness. An idealized traditional rural life was repackaged for a commercial market. For example, the daily food of poor peasants, such as barley rice bowls, buckwheat noodles, broiled potatoes, and young radish kimchi, is now packaged as well-being delights and served at trendy restaurants in Seoul. Well-being is increasingly understood as something to be achieved by consuming "health foods" and using all kinds of health-promoting products such as *welbing* rice cookers and juice makers, modern air purifiers, humidifiers, and exercise machines. Such products used to be imported from the United States, Japan, and Europe. They are now produced by Korean manufacturers, but the well-being culture is still closely associated with Western-style middle-class life, as demonstrated in yoga ads featuring an attractive Western actress and in a real estate commercial featuring a happy middle-class family enjoying an outdoor barbecue in a country-style villa.

These products are not just for show. Global capital mobilizes cutting-edge science and technology to produce high value–added products that promise a more comfortable, healthy, and luxurious life. Moving beyond conspicuous consumption and ostentatious lifestyles, today's wealthy people can buy products that actually are life-enhancing, including new medicines and drugs, healthy foods, safer vehicles, air purifiers, and many other things that are supposed to protect them from the risk society. So, it is not just lifestyle but also the actual quality of life that can be changed by money.

The well-being boom has also seen a revival of interest in Korea's traditional foods and indigenous methods of exercise and health maintenance, just as the luxury goods market spawned a reawakening of interest in the artifacts and practices of traditional Korean culture. This is partly due to the realization that many of the foods that Koreans used to eat—back when they were a lot poorer—are actually very healthy. Along with simple peasant foods on the menus of fashionable restaurants in Seoul, all kinds of local Korean wine have been revived, as have many other forgotten health-nourishing foods. Tea drinking in the traditional manner has reappeared in higher social circles as well.

In this revival of traditional health practices, we see the same nationalistic reaction to Western cultural influences that led to the revival of traditional wedding and funeral ceremonies (Kendall 1996). Yet Korean people's growing preference for national or indigenous products is particularly noticeable in the realm of food. This is largely due to the influx of cheap agricultural and meat products imported from China, America, and Australia. After the trade liberalization in the 1990s the volume of agricultural imports increased tremendously, but Koreans soon realized that domestically grown products tasted better and were of more reliable quality. (This is due, of course, to importers who bring in low-quality, cheaper products for market reasons.) Those who can afford to therefore prefer to eat domestically produced goods despite the higher prices. Reputable restaurants are expected to use only domestically produced meats. The label "Produced in Korea" carries a high value in restaurants and supermarkets. The dominant ethos expressed in this cultural response is "ours is the best." A popular slogan that appeared in the 1990s is *sinto buri* (body and soil cannot be separated), implying that whatever grows in the soil of one's own land is the most wholesome and nourishing.

This new awareness of the superiority of domestic products encouraged many Korean farmers to start producing high-quality organic products for upper-income customers. The price difference between these premium-quality products and ordinary ones is large and growing larger. The fishery market shows the same trend. As many of the preferred eating fishes have declined sharply in supply, some, such as *kalchi* (cutlassfish) and *gulbi* (corvina), have become too expensive for ordinary people to enjoy anymore. Some of these high-end agricultural and fishery products are labeled *myongpoom* (or even "aristocratic") products, and they are often sold through individualized marketing channels targeted at the rich. Today, most classy department stores have their premium-class food corners that display organic vegetables, premium-quality fishes and meats, and a variety of Western foods such as olive oil, cheeses, and cured meats. Also displayed prominently are special-quality soybean sauces, soybean pastes, red pepper pastes, and the like that are produced by artisans who claim to be heirs of certain well-known families in Korea's culinary world.

The well-being consumption market for well-off people is enabled by Korea's superefficient home-delivery system. In today's Korea, almost anything can be obtained quickly through home delivery by motorcycles, which zip through the congested city traffic. The well-to-do can sit at home and enjoy all kinds of foods prepared with specially produced rice, soybean products, fruits, seasonal fishes, or traditional medicinal products delivered straight to their doors. They can also have these things custom-produced. Many well-to-do families have direct contact with vegetable producers and fishery companies in the countryside and have their favorite foods home-delivered directly. The transition of Korean agriculture and fishery industries to more high value–added production means a more privileged lifestyle for the rich and greater relative deprivation for the poor. The business of delivering prepared foods has also recently become diversified with high-end options. In the past it was relatively inexpensive popular foods, such as Chinese noodles, *jjajangmyon*, and pizza, that were delivered to homes, but now some companies specialize in delivering top-quality ready-made foods prepared by first-class cooks and packaged immaculately. A leading company in this area in 2020 is Market Kurly, which takes orders until 11:00 p.m. and delivers the food to the client's door by 7:00 a.m. the next day. In addition to foods, of course, all kinds of consumer goods, such as clothes, utensils, toys, hobby materials, and so on, are also delivered in a superefficient manner. Thus, in many ways, the rise of well-being culture in Korea has widened class differences between the haves and the have-nots. And we can find widening differentials occurring within the larger middle class between the affluent segment and the rest of the middle. In terms of both lifestyle and life chances, the affluent and privileged segment of the middle class is slowly separating itself from the ordinary middle class.

What needs to be noted about the popularity of well-being culture in Korea is that this commercially driven lifestyle is essentially individualistic and escapist. It is all about seeking a better quality of life for oneself and one's immediate family, with little concern for the community as a whole or for the environmental consequences of such a lifestyle. While growing concern with health and well-being in the West has occurred in conjunction with the environmental and sustainability movements (e.g., the Slow Food movement in Italy, the Downshift movement in England, and the LOHAS, or lifestyles of health and sustainability, movement in the United States), it is hard to find a similar environmental consciousness among rich consumers in Korea. At this stage of Korean development, the new rich are more interested in securing their class privilege and status distinction than in community welfare or public well-being.

Beyond *Myongpoom*

Entering the 2000s, we saw many changes in Korea's luxury consumption market. Today, *myongpoom* goods abound and are easily accessible and even sold online and through mail-order systems. But a luxury good can only maintain its value so long as it remains exclusive. A Louis Vuitton bag can bring status to its holder when a select few can possess it, but when counterfeits abound and can be seen in the hands of grocery shoppers in neighborhood supermarkets, its distinct value as a status symbol is bound to be lost. It is apparent that Korea in the early twenty-first century has achieved the "democratization of luxury" that other advanced economies have experienced before (Currid-Halkett 2017).

A new trend that appeared among the rich in the 2000s was thus to move beyond the obsession with conventional *myongpoom* goods. One way to do this is to go for the more expensive and exclusive grades produced by brand-name producers. The luxury industries constantly upgrade and differentiate their products to meet the desires of various categories of customers. Wealthier customers look down on the usual brand-name goods with a logo distinctly displayed on them and instead prefer luxury goods that display their premier quality in a more subtle way and with more discretely placed logos. But their preferred approach is to acquire things that are rarer altogether and less accessible to ordinary middle-class people. The younger and globally mobile members of the rich are eager to discover products that are popular among cultured people in some localities in Europe or other continents. These are things that ordinary middle-class people are unaware of and have no appreciation of, but they have a special value in status competition among inner circles of affluent friends and acquaintances. Discovering and possessing these things requires more than money; it also requires information, frequent overseas travel, and the ability to discern quality. What we observe in today's Korea thus parallels changing consumption patterns among the rich in the United States and Europe. As Currid-Halkett (2017) observes, new elites are consuming fewer conventional conspicuous items and instead look to more subtle status markers, which include less conspicuous but more exclusive goods as well as certain lifestyle elements requiring more money.

This change is partly due to the arrival of the second generation of the new rich. The younger generation is more globally educated and globally mobile than their parents and therefore possess more cosmopolitan tastes in their consumption and leisure activities. Many of them have knowledge of and access to current fashions in New York, Paris, London, and Milan. Such knowledge, along with firsthand experience of diverse cultures and the ability to discern and enjoy foreign foods, music, and arts, has become the new status symbol. That is, a certain degree of cosmopolitanism has become an important part of upper-middle-class culture.

Cosmopolitanism is originally an ethical and philosophical notion, referring to "an intellectual and aesthetic stance of openness toward divergent cultural experience" (Hannerz 1990, 239) or a philosophical commitment to the ideal that "as members of humanity, all persons are in a fundamental sense equal and free and deserve equal political treatment regardless of their origin" (Guibernau 2008, 148). But cosmopolitanism also has a more mundane meaning. In popular understanding, "cosmopolitans" often refer to those who travel a lot and are familiar with and open to other cultures. Along with the swift toward globalization of the Korean economy over recent decades, cosmopolitanism has gained cultural value in Korean society. While cosmopolitanism does involve cultural diversity and openness to the Other as an important moral and political value orientation, in actual life it puts more emphasis on the cultural competence implied in the concept such as foreign language ability (especially English competence), the cultural taste and knowledge gained from many overseas trips or study abroad, and the ability to be comfortable in foreign settings or dealing with foreigners. Rather than an ethical principle of openness to Others, then, it is this cosmopolitanism as a lifestyle that increasingly differentiates the upper middle class from the ordinary middle class. Increasingly, a certain cosmopolitan aura is required for acceptance in elite circles in Korea today. This is particularly noticeable in the wealthy neighborhoods of Gangnam such as Chungdamdong, Apgujeongdong, and Samsungdong. In fact, while it was the affluent residents of

Gangnam who led the *myongpoom* phenomenon, they are now trying to leave it behind to their mass followers while they themselves seek a more refined and cosmopolitan style of living as a critical mark of class distinction between themselves and the ordinary middle class.

The Body as a Status Symbol

Another important cultural trend today is Korean people's obsession with physical appearance. Increasingly, the idea of luxury and high status is extended to health and body appearance. If the earlier practices of luxury consumption were satisfied with simple possession and display of luxury goods, the new trend stresses the bodily consumption of fashionable goods and bodily expression of the results of consuming these products. The upper middle class must show their high status not simply by possessing luxury goods but also by consuming them differently and effectively through their well-trimmed bodies. As Liechty (2003, 143) argues, "Being fashionable is about more than simply what you have; it is also about how you use it, how you carry it off."

Of course, physical appearance is important in any society, and Korea may be no exception in this regard. But the amount of emphasis Koreans put on appearance as a measure of self-esteem and social status and the amount of effort individuals make to look good are extraordinary indeed. As described in the *Chosun Daily* newspaper, "Koreans of all ages are obsessed with their looks and will go to almost any length, from punishing fitness regimes to plastic surgery, to ensure they are attractive. Behind their obsession lies the collective consciousness that appearance determines success or failure in life. The phenomenon could cause people to lose self-esteem and view themselves entirely as objects" (Chosun Ilbo English 2005).

Why, then, are Koreans so obsessed with appearance? A quick answer is that many Koreans do indeed believe that their looks will affect their success or failure in the job market as well as in dating and marriage choices. While appearance matters in these domains in all modern societies, today's Koreans seem to have a somewhat stronger belief that their appearance determines their life's trajectory and therefore are willing to invest a lot of money and effort in their looks. It is partly related to Korea's corporate culture that until recently treated female employees largely as a secondary workforce, almost like flowers in the office, and stressed their appearance and pleasant demeanor as primary criteria of selection. But this kind of cultural explanation is insufficient. We must realize that Koreans' obsession with appearance is a recent phenomenon, something that has grown strong as Korea has become a highly developed consumerist society.

Thus, we need to consider factors related to the development of Korea's consumer industry in recent decades.

Korea is widely known for its highly developed cosmetic surgery industry and the large numbers of young people who have had cosmetic surgery. Some reports estimate that half of Korean women in their twenties have received some kind of plastic surgery (Chadha and Husband 2006, 262). Thus, it may not be absurd that foreign media often insinuate that the main reason why almost all Korean actresses and actors and K-pop performers are good-looking is thanks to receiving some kind of sophisticated plastic surgery. Though not flattering, this kind of reputation helps the Korean beauty industry draw thousands of tourists from China, Japan, and Southeast Asian countries every year whose primary purpose is to receive plastic surgery in Korea. Many of these visitors are said to bring with them images of their favorite K-pop stars whom they hope to resemble.

Along with cosmetic surgery, Korea's beauty industry offers excellent services in skin care and body maintenance. While those in their twenties are more likely to seek cosmetic surgeries of some kind, middle-aged women are more interested in cosmetic services for slowing the effects of aging on their skin and body shape. The large amounts of money and time spent on these services are attested by the ubiquitous presence of cosmetic surgery and skin care clinics in Korean cities, especially in the Gangnam area. And the wealthier the district, the fancier and more numerous are its beauty clinics. The overdeveloped beauty industry subjects Korean consumers to tremendous amounts of advertisement, including a bombardment of aggressive and sophisticated ads for plastic surgery, skin care, weight control, special diets, hair implants, and so on. Having become one of the most wired populations in the world, Koreans spend an enormous amount of time on the Internet, with their smartphones, and watching TV, all of which carry a continuous stream of ads stoking the appetite for beauty-enhancing products and services. With the development of Korea's powerful beauty industry, a new cultural idea about physical beauty has been introduced. This is the idea that one's appearance is not determined at birth but instead is something to be shaped and reshaped by one's own efforts and with the help of modern technology. This notion of the plasticity of our bodies and faces puts the responsibility for good looks or bad looks on the individuals and encourages them to seek surgical help to achieve a good appearance.

Another factor that has influenced Korean people's preoccupation with appearance is the country's success in popularizing Korean TV dramas and popular dance music abroad, the so-called *hallyu* (Korean wave). One of the main reasons for the *hallyu* success abroad is its presentation of a sleek, modern, affluent life in an Asian setting along with a host of good-looking performers. Skillfully presented in these products is an Asian form of modernity that differs from the one represented by the American Hollywood style. The producers are aware of this kind of attraction to foreign audiences and try to maximize such an effect. The performers are selected by the industry and trained judiciously for many years before appearing in front of audiences (Hong 2014). Apparently, this strategy has worked well to produce the *hallyu* success. But an important consequence of *hallyu* popularity, both inside and outside of Korea, has been to raise the standard for good looks among Koreans. With the saturated images of *hallyu* stars on television and Internet screens, their Western-looking faces and body styles have become a norm to be followed. Many young people, both Korean and non-Korean, want to have their faces look as much like the faces of their *hallyu*-star idols as possible. Thus, Korea's eagerness to present itself to the outside world as a country of cool culture filled with trendy, good-looking people has contributed to inducing Koreans to become preoccupied with their own looks in order to be proper members of this fictitious society.

Having emphasized some unique features of the Korean obsession with appearance and fashionable lifestyles, we need to put Korea in a comparative perspective. In fact, what we observe in Korea today reflects what is becoming a dominant trend in the West, especially in the United States. Of course, the wellbeing or wellness culture in Europe and the United States is much older. In the West, it emerged as an alternative to the excessively materialist and consumerist culture and advocated a slower nonmaterialist and sustainable lifestyle. Yet the ideas and language of these movements have been quickly appropriated by commercial interests and used to promote a wide range of products, including expensive organic vegetables, all kinds of health foods, and other health-enhancing products targeting well-off consumers. Devotees of wellness culture in America and Europe are preoccupied with exercise, health, and body maintenance. Eating healthy foods, exercising rigorously, and staying fit are the distinguishing characteristics of the lifestyle, which can be enjoyed most easily by affluent people. The trend has only intensified in recent years. As one fashion magazine commentator writes, "Wellness certainly doesn't come cheap in the modern day world. From $180 a month gym memberships to $10 cold-pressed juices, from $500 personal trainers to $30 weekly classes, the price of natural, organic and healthy products and services keeps increasing with every passing year. Most people find such exorbitant spending to be preposterous, but many high net worth individuals also find it to be an integral part of their luxury lifestyle" (*Oro Gold Cosmetics* 2015).

Analysts of consumption trends in America seem to agree that an important change occurred in the wellness market after the global financial crisis of 2007–2008. Luxury shoppers became more reluctant to purchase goods that actively flaunted their wealth and instead began to spend more on exercise, sport, travel, and extravagant experiences. As a spinning enthusiast quoted in *Vogue* commented, "'You are a douche if you brag about your car or how much money you make, but bragging about how much you spin is normal, though still very annoying'" (qtd. in Phelan 2015). What is important is not necessarily the kind of exercise one is doing but rather where one is doing it and in what kind of outfit. As an editorial director for a lifestyle website describes, "'What you wear to yoga class and the kind of mat you carry has become as important as the kind of class you take'" (qtd. in Stelio 2015). The larger trend we can read in the wellness boom in the twenty-first century is the increasing focus on the body as a major object or means of class distinction. An expert of consumer marketing said that "'people are investing in themselves as a product. As well as having the flash outfit, they want to have the flash body that goes with it'" (qtd. in Stelio 2015).

These shrewd observations made by marketing experts in the United States, Australia, and elsewhere make us see that what is happening in Korea's consumption patterns is more or less a copy of the Western trend. There seems to be nothing unique about Koreans' obsession with appearance; they are simply following the common trend found in the advanced industrial societies. But one interesting difference is that while American middle-class people exercise in order to achieve body fitness, their Korean counterparts invest a lot more in maintaining youthful-looking faces and skin. While exercise and gym membership, especially in luxurious health clubs, do serve as important status symbols for affluent Koreans, the dominant trend in Korea thus far is choosing an easier and more passive approach, that is, trying to achieve the desired physical appearance through cosmetic services rather than strenuous exercise. This difference may be due to cultural factors, such as Korea's emphasis on facial beauty over body fitness, but perhaps a more important reason might be the overdevelopment of the beauty industry in Korea, which provides easy access to high-quality cosmetic services and an easier solution to appearance maintenance. Thus, money appears to play a more important role in determining one's physical appearance in Korea than in America and Europe, simply because cosmetic services are more easily available and of high quality at a lower cost than in the West.

Changing Reference Group

Robert Frank (2007, 5) argues that "rising inequality harms the middle class." The way this occurs is through the rising expenditures that the middle class is compelled to make to keep up with the rising consumption standard that is introduced by the rich. "As incomes continue to grow at the top and stagnate elsewhere, we will see even more of your national income devoted to luxury goods, the main effect of which will be to raise the bar that defines what counts as luxury" (102).

In every society, it is the rich or near-rich who lead consumption patterns. They are often engaged in conspicuous consumption in order to distinguish themselves from the rest of the population. This is not a new phenomenon but instead is quite old and historical, as Veblen (1967) wrote such an insightful book about it. What is new today is that people's reference groups have changed. In the old days, people's main reference group was their neighbors, who would be similar in economic status or slightly richer or poorer than themselves. So, "keeping up with the Joneses" did not require too great of a stretch in one's spending. But in the contemporary world, people's reference groups have moved up quite high. As Juliet Schor (1998, 4) describes, "the comparisons we make are no longer restricted to those in our own general earnings category, or even to those one rung above us on the ladder. Today a person is more likely to be making comparisons with, or choose as a 'reference group,' people whose incomes are three, four, or five times his or her own. The result is that millions of us have become participants in a national culture of upscale spending. I call it the new consumerism."

This new consumerism or, more accurately, competitive upscale consumption is what we also observe in Korea. This has occurred since the 1990s with the liberalization and globalization of the Korean economy and with the increasing concentration of income and wealth at the top. But a unique feature of Korea's upscale consumption is that it has developed in close connection with the development of Gangnam as an upper-middle–class town. The concentration of well-to-do people in one large area and their relatively homogeneous upscale lifestyle created a visible reference group for the mass of middle-class people, a reference group that looks to be successful, powerful, and enjoying the good life. If in the old days the Korean middle class learned about cultural standards from the distant reference group of the American middle class, they now learn from Gangnam's rich and successful.

4
CLASS MAKING, GANGNAM STYLE

Psy's megahit dance song "Gangnam Style" brought celebrity status to a newly developed area of Seoul. Gangnam, which means "south of the river," represents the southern half of metropolitan Seoul. Gangnam is a freshly made, ultramodern, world-class city that within a span of three decades arose in what had been a large area of paddy fields. A product of state-led, compressed urban development, Gangnam possesses no recognizable landmarks, no sculptures of its famous people, no traditional cultural sites, no buildings older than fifty years of age, and, in short, no historical memory. Instead, it has world-class department stores, fancy restaurants and cafés, fashionable boutique shops, cool jazz bars, top-notch hospitals, plenty of cosmetic surgery centers and skin care clinics, and many luxurious high-rise apartments, which make the whole area look like a huge apartment forest.

Every country in the world has areas that can be identified as wealthy or upper middle class, but few have such a large-scale congregation of economically and socially homogeneous middle-class residents in one contiguous space. Although not every area of Gangnam is affluent, its three core districts (Gangnamgu, Seochogu, and Songpagu) are definitely middle or upper middle class in terms of the residents' economic status. In 2010, these three core districts had a resident population of 1.6 million, comprising 15 percent of the entire population of metropolitan Seoul and about 3 percent of the national population.

In popular discussions, the Gangnam style is talked about mainly as a lifestyle—that of being sleek, fashionable, fun-loving, flamboyant, and somewhat hedonistic. But Gangnam represents more than a lifestyle or a popular culture.

It also represents a particular way in which a new affluent and privileged class segment has been produced through the authoritarian state's large-scale urban project and the ways this affluent class has developed its unique class culture. In this chapter, I focus on the Gangnam style of class making and its impact on shaping middle-class culture in Korea.

Gangnam's Development

The idea of developing a large area south of the Han River first arose in the 1960s, mainly as a possible solution to the problem of Seoul's overcrowding. By the late 1960s, large-scale migration from the countryside was overwhelming Seoul's ability to absorb more people. Infrastructure was inadequate, housing was in short supply, and the arteries of the city were congested. While several proposals to expand to the south were made during the 1960s, development of the Gangnam area began in earnest in the early 1970s. By that time several key infrastructure developments were either completed or under construction, including the Seoul-Busan cross-country highway system and the Third Han River Bridge, which were soon followed by more bridges and tunnels connecting the north and south banks of the river. Another factor, however, was military consideration (Ji 2017). In the event of an invasion by North Korea, which had always been a keen concern of the military government in South Korea, having three million people concentrated on the north side of the Han River would be a liability. This concern was heightened by a North Korean commando attack on the presidential palace in an attempted assassination of President Park Chung Hee in 1968.

Once the Park government decided to redistribute Seoul's population, it embarked on the construction of the new city in a typical militaristic, authoritarian style (Gelézeau 2007).[1] The government began by appropriating land from private owners at extremely low prices. Prior to its development, Gangnam was largely paddy fields, low-value orchid farms, and scattered villages of poor farming households. The land had little commercial value, and the inhabitants had no power to oppose the government's urban development plan. Thus, the government enjoyed a completely free hand as it drew up the development plans. There is no evidence that the planners gave any serious attention to aesthetics, ecological impacts, or social balance with other parts of the country. Instead, their main concern was to build a large modern-style new city in the fastest and most effective method possible—a city that would sufficiently augment Seoul's housing and business facilities and provide a fitting image for the miraculous development of the Korean economy (the so-called Miracle on the Han River).

Along with heavy investment in the area's infrastructure, the government employed several policy measures to induce people and businesses to move into the newly built area. First, several major government offices were relocated to Gangnam from Gangbuk (the area north of the Han River), including the Supreme Court, the Supreme Prosecutor's Office, the Bureau of Trade and Tourism, and the Korean Customs Service. The government also offered various tax incentives to private developers. When these measures failed to inspire enough businesses to relocate in the south, the government enacted the Gangbuk Suppression Policies, which disallowed the opening in Gangbuk of several categories of new businesses, including entertainment venues, wholesale companies, factories, and department stores.

But probably the most effective measure the Park government adopted to encourage middle-class residents to move to Gangnam was to have several old elite high schools relocate from Gangbuk. This was the period of the Park government's draconian High School Equalization Policy, which was an attempt to address the excessive competition for entrance into the elite high schools. As a consequence of this radical policy, previously elite high schools lost their prestige and competitive merits. But by moving to the affluent area of Gangnam, these institutions gained a chance to revive their reputations and at the same time increased the property values of the area. In fact, in the 1970s Gangnam was still an underdeveloped place with poor infrastructural services and inconvenient transportation, and most middle-class families were hesitant to move to this uncertain area. Only those who were financially smart and alert and read the real estate market trend faster than others were more willing to move there. But with the relocation of elite schools to Gangnam, the middle-class perception of this fledgling city changed noticeably. Gangnam emerged as a land of opportunity not only in speculative real estate investment but also in children's education. These two powerful incentives worked together to accelerate population growth in Gangnam from the 1980s.

One of the most distinct aspects of Gangnam as a residential area is that it is largely made of apartments. Single houses are rare, and apartment buildings fill the view in all directions. In the early 1980s, apartments made up 76 percent of all housing built in Gangnam. The same is true of many other Korean cities today because they tried to copy the Gangnam pattern. So numerous and so popular are apartments in South Korea that a French urban geographer, Gelézeau (2007), aptly called the country "the Republic of Apartments." From the very beginning of Gangnam's development, policymakers have preferred massive numbers of apartments to single-family homes because apartment construction is the fastest and most cost-effective way of providing new housing to many consumers. Another important reason for their popularity, however, is their attraction for

FIGURE 4.1. Map of Seoul

Source: Korea's National Geographic Information Institute (redrawn by Kyoung Jin Kim).

the middle class, especially middle-class housewives. Living in an apartment equipped with modern-style kitchens, bathrooms, and living rooms meant leading a comfortable middle-class life.

Speculative Real Estate Investment

The amazing speed of land transformation and housing construction in the state-managed Gangnam development project gave rise to a host of unanticipated problems. The most serious of these had to do with the real estate market. Land prices in the area skyrocketed but did so unevenly and erratically. Those who were financially alert and politically connected were able to anticipate what was coming; these people purchased land in the most profitable areas of Gangnam and reaped huge profits. Gangnam thus became a land of tremendous speculative investment activity. Although some of the previous landowners benefited from this development, those who profited the most are the ones who had large amounts of capital and the political connections to obtain information about the government's urban development plan before it became public. Many chaebol groups purchased large pieces of land in Gangnam well before prices went up and have kept them as a major source of reserved capital (Son 2003). Another player in this speculative real estate game was the Park government itself.[2]

Apart from these large players, Gangnam's development provided opportunities for many ordinary individuals who were financially minded and had money to invest. Between 1963 and 1979 Gangnam land prices increased by 800–1,300 times, while in a typical district in Gangbuk (Yongsan) they increased by 25 times (Cho 2004). The state's deep intervention in the real estate market was largely responsible for encouraging these heated speculative investment activities. With the good intention of controlling the prices of the newly built apartments, the government set a price limit that was lower than market value and selected buyer applicants through a lottery system (Yang 2018a). Whenever a new apartment building was under construction, the lucky lottery winners would receive an advance contract. But oddly, the contract holders were allowed to sell the contracts to other buyers at full market value within a year or two, even before construction was completed. These irregularities stimulated speculative real estate investment throughout the 1980s and 1990s. Because the applicants for new apartments were required to meet certain financial qualifications, virtually all of them were middle-class people. In addition, the application process was unwieldy and required a fair time investment, with the result that the majority of those who were actively engaged in the real estate market, at least on the surface, were middle-class housewives. These women became the focus of a great deal of social attention. They were called *bok buin* (luck-seeking housewives or "Mrs. Realtor") and were often portrayed in the media as investment-speculating villains.

More and more middle-class residents moved from Gangbuk to Gangnam in the 1980s. Even many of those conservative people who found no favor for the overly commercialized and flashy-looking district were eventually persuaded to move to Gangnam purely for their children's education. The rising prices benefited those who had made the move early on, regardless of whether their motivation had been financial gain or educational opportunity.[3] In contrast, those families who were more attached to their old neighborhoods in Gangbuk or had no ready money to purchase a newly built apartment in Gangnam had to experience substantial financial loss compared to those who moved to Gangnam early on. Thus, a divergence developed in the family fortunes of the middle class depending on where they had decided to reside, Gangnam or Gangbuk. Needless to say, those who lived in the countryside experienced an even greater relative loss in the value of their property than homeowners in any part of Seoul (Ji 2017; Yang 2018a).

Gangnam Culture

At the beginning of Gangnam's development, the people who gave a distinct character to this area's cultural atmosphere were those who were making tremendous profits from speculative real estate investment in the area. The first district to be developed was Youngdong, which in the late 1970s was populated most visibly by hundreds of real estate offices and rows of restaurants, bars, dance halls, and other places of entertainment. This area was well known for its many expensive hostess bars where real estate brokers liked to entertain their customers and bureaucrats. The Young-dong culture, as depicted in the media at that time, was predominantly a culture of money, sex, and pleasure—a highly materialistic, hedonist, and opportunistic culture.

As Gangnam grew into an affluent middle-class apartment district in the 1980s, its vulgar, hedonistic image became gradually attenuated but did not completely disappear. By the mid-1980s, Apgujeongdong and Sinsadong appeared as new centers of Gangnam life. While Sinsadong's image was somewhat similar to that of Young-dong as a pleasure-seeking place of eating, drinking, and entertainment, Apgujeongdong became a fashionable shopping district that exemplified a luxurious lifestyle, setting the dominant tone of the emerging consumerist culture of Gangnam. In the 1990s when Korea's economic liberalization relaxed control over luxury imports, Apgujeongdong became a leading center of the so-called *myongpoom* craze. This is the area where the first two grand-scale luxury apartment complexes (Banpo and Hyundai apartments) were built by conglomerate firms to attract well-to-do families. The Hyundai group also established two luxury department stores on the main streets of Apgujeongdong (Hyundai Department Store and the Galeria), which specialize in brand-name imports for rich clients. In the 2000s, the Samsung conglomerate opened its own top-class department store, Silla, in the area. In addition, Apgujeongdong has its own Rodeo Drive, mimicking the original in Beverly Hills with all kinds of luxury brand stores, fancy restaurants, and trendy cafés and bars.

In the 2000s the center of fashion and luxurious consumption moved to Chungdamdong, which had more luxurious apartments and more sophisticated restaurants, bars, and entertainment places than Apgujeongdong. In addition, Chungdamdong drew in many cultural activities from Gangbuk, such as art galleries, film studios, architects' offices, book cafés, antique furniture shops, and the like. The neighborhood also became well known for high-end cosmetic surgery and skin care services.

Gangnam's spatial development was not, however, entirely unidirectional. The area has also seen diversification in the activities and subcultures it represents. Beyond the main belt connecting Apgujeongdong and Chungdamdong, one popular consumption space has developed around the Gangnam subway station. Filled by numerous restaurants, cafés, beer halls, karaoke rooms, and the like, this area provides an alternative space for low-income youths. In the 2000s, another important space opened in the eastern section of Gangnam with the construction of a huge entertainment and dining complex called the Samsung Co-ex Mall, which provides an enormously popular entertainment place for teenagers and other young people.

These sociospatial developments testify to the continuous expansion and diversification of the Gangnam culture and lifestyle. Nevertheless, "Gangnam style" retains its posh connotations. The Korean media has given intensive attention to the consumption patterns and lifestyle associated with the area. Gangnam style represents a product of this media construction as much as reality. The media has consistently taken a critical attitude toward Gangnam's consumption culture, reflecting the generally negative images that non-Gangnam people hold of Gangnam people. The media's descriptions of Gangnam were studded with such terms as "real estate," "luxury," "overconsumption," and "distorted consumption culture" (Kang 2004; Lee 2017; Lee and Lee 2017; Bae and Joo 2019). Literary writers also expressed highly critical views of Gangnam's consumerist culture, describing it as dystopic, hedonistic, decadent, and generally a center of vulgar capitalism (see Kang 2004). While such negative views of Gangnam have endured, a closer look reveals a subtle but important change over time. In a very instructive analysis of the changing pattern of media representations of Gangnam, Young Min Lee (2017) describes four stages of Gangnam's cultural change as perceived by the media and the public.

Stage one is the early period of Gangnam's development in the 1970s. This is the period when speculative real estate activities in the area received most of the media's attention. The media propagated an extremely negative image of Youngdong as a materialistic and hedonistic entertainment neighborhood patronized by real estate speculators. In addition, the term *bok buin* was coined and frequently used by the media during this period.

Stage two runs from the 1980s to the early 1990s, when Apgujeongdong emerged as the center of luxury consumption and high fashion. This is also the period after the 1987 democratization and the 1988 Seoul Olympic Games. Economic liberalization stimulated consumption overall, but it was Apgujeongdong that led luxury consumption. The media and the intellectual community were somewhat alarmed by the vulgar, pleasure-seeking consumer culture exploding in this area and often described Gangnam as a "hotspot of luxury and overconsumption."

Stage three covers the mid-1990s to the early 2000s. This was a period of maturation and diversification of Gangnam's popular culture. Gangnam's consumption culture moved beyond Apgujeongdong to new areas, especially Chungdamdong, which took over the title of the most affluent neighborhood, and the Gangnam subway station area and Samsung Co-ex Mall, which developed as lower-end consuming spaces for younger and low-income consumers. With this expansion and diversification of Gangnam culture and style, the media began to look at it a little differently, dialing down its criticism and beginning to "look at Gangnam as a place of diverse forms of high-class consumption culture rather than just a place of luxury and overconsumption" (Lee 2017, 73).

Stage four refers to the early 2000s to present, when Gangnam's consumption culture has further expanded and diversified and the media's critique of Gangnam culture has continued to soften and grow more nuanced. Media commentators began to recognize Gangnam culture not as peculiar or limited to this area but rather as representative of the general trend of the nation's consumption culture. Commercial interests began to look at Gangnam as a testing ground for new products and fashions. Even when critics disapprove of Gangnam culture, their target has shifted from its conspicuous consumption to its exclusiveness; the charge now is that affluent Gangnam residents are trying to maintain their own (exclusive) space of consumption and cultural activities. The media critique is no longer focused on the idea that Gangnam culture is too materialistic or hedonistic and instead is increasingly focused on the fact that this cultural space is becoming monopolized by wealthy residents of Gangnam. Expressed in most media comments is an implicit acceptance or admiration of Gangnam style mixed with dissatisfaction that this fashionable culture has become the exclusive domain of the affluent and privileged.

Class Formation, Gangnam Style

As we have seen, Gangnam has from the beginning been a primarily middle-class town. Most apartments built in Gangnam have targeted middle-income or more well-to-do buyers. The soaring price of housing has greatly increased the assets of residents while placing entry into the area even further out of reach of lower-middle–class families. The popular image of Gangnam as a place of wealthy residents is not ungrounded. This is clearly an area where a disproportionate number of rich are living, measured by statistics on their possessions and tax rates as well as apartment prices.[4]

A more important fact is that Gangnam is the place where Korea's power elites congregate to live. According to one analysis, Gangnam is the residence of a surprisingly large proportion of Korean elites: 61.3 percent of the nation's lawyers, 56.4 percent of the doctors, 54 percent of the entrepreneurs, 52.8 percent of the financial managers, 50.2 percent of the civil servants, and 36.2 percent of the journalists (Cho 2004). Given the fact that the Gangnam population accounts for about 15 percent of Seoul's population in the early 2000s, there is clearly an overrepresentation of power elites in this particular area.

Thus, many critical scholars look at Gangnam as the birthplace of the new affluent middle class in Korea (Cho 2004; Kang 2004; Kang 2006; Son 2008; Shin 2013; Park and Chang 2017). As Myung Rae Cho (2004, 33) eloquently describes, "Gangnam has become a (biblical) boat in which Korea's new upper class came to put its nest." Similarly, Nae Hee Kang (2004, 72) argues that "Gangnam is a space where the dominant class alliance enjoys a privileged status through exclusive control over social investments and resources." Of course, not all residents of Gangnam are rich or part of the professional and managerial class, and some low-income families live in scattered spots. Moreover, many Gangnam residents today complain of their vulnerable financial situation due to forced early retirement, the rising cost of living, and the continued burden of expensive education. But it is also true that most people who live in Gangnam were motivated to move there by the desire to enjoy the many advantages offered by the area and the status recognition associated with Gangnam residence, so most residents may well share common interests and common outlooks. We therefore could look at Gangnam as a special geographical area where a new distinct segment of the upper middle class has been formed. This segment represents a subset rather than the entire upper middle class in Korea. But the way Gangnam's new upper-middle–class segment was formed and the distinct social character it came to possess have huge ramifications for Korean society as a whole, which is why examining its nature closely is important.

The most distinguishing aspect of Gangnam's affluent middle class is that its material basis was real estate investment in the area during the period of rapid housing development. Whether they actively participated in speculative real estate investment or not, everyone who moved to Gangnam early enough benefited enormously by owning a property (or properties) in Gangnam. There is thus wide agreement among Korean scholars in identifying Gangnam's affluent class primarily in terms of wealth formation through speculative real estate investment. Cho (2004, 29), for example, argues that "speculative wealth produced by Gangnam land was offered indiscriminately to those who moved to this area and provided a material base for the rise of Korea's middle and upper classes." Ji (2017, 187) similarly argues that "the material base for the middle- and upper-class Gangnam residents is basically their real estate ownership." Looking at Gangnam as a peculiar form of urban development, Park (2017, 9) argue that "in the end, Gangnam-ization led to forming the Korean urban middle class as an agent of speculative investment who depends on the increasing value of real estate, and this fact contributed to making the speculative investment-oriented urban development the dominant urban paradigm in Korea." In a similar vein, Yang (2018a, 137) argues that "the current fragility of the middle class was deeply embedded in the speculative and exclusionary ways in which it was formed during the era of high economic growth."

The main reason why the property value of Gangnam has continuously increased is that the state has invested heavily in this area and tried to make Gangnam the most modern global city. At the outset, the state constructed many bridges to connect the north and south of metropolitan Seoul and invested heavily in making Gangnam the hub of the national transportation system. When the subway system was developed beginning in the 1970s, the state ensured that most of the lines passed through Gangnam. Gangnam thus came to have more subway lines and stations than other districts in Seoul, and Gangnam's were also better equipped. In addition, from the beginning the state tried to lay down the infrastructure suitable for a model district. Thus, Gangnam is more modern and functional than any other district in Korea with a more modern landscape, more green space, wider and straighter roads, better electricity and sewage systems, more convenient connections to the subway system, and so on. Gangnam is also endowed with many cultural and sports facilities such as concert halls, an opera house, galleries, libraries, and the Olympic stadium. Even the number of public libraries (per number of residents) is much larger than in Gangbuk. Local governments in Gangnam districts are financially well endowed and thus able to provide much better social welfare services and cultural programs to their residents than Gangbuk can. More important, Gangnam has become more than a center of fashion and luxury consumption; it is also the nerve center for high-tech industry and venture capitalism, especially in telecommunications, entertainment, and advertising. Many Korean conglomerate firms have their headquarters in Gangnam, which it also draws many international financial firms (banks, insurance firms, investment and accounting services) and flagship stores of global brand-name products. Thus, in many ways Gangnam has become a full-fledged global city, and its global influence is growing fast. This means that Gangnam residents enjoy more job market advantages especially in terms of access to more desirable professional and technical jobs in the global sector.

Probably a more important factor that has kept the real estate value of Gangnam continuously increasing and made this area so preferable to live in is the educational advantages it provides to middle-class families. In fact, Gangnam's development cannot be separated from the extremely competitive educational environment in Korea. As described above, the Park Chung Hee government used the relocation of old elite high schools from Gangbuk to Gangnam to induce many middle-class families to move to this new area at the early stage of its development. Concentration of these old elite schools in the affluent areas of Gangnam, later known as the eighth educational district, established Gangnam as the most desirable educational district in the nation. But the establishment of a privileged district of public high schools was only the beginning. Affluent middle-class parents wanted to have more diverse and effective means to prepare their children to be more competitive. Thus, all kinds of cram schools, private institutes, and tutorial services have appeared. Given the wealth of the area, Gangnam attracted the best quality of private education, which helps a disproportionate number of Gangnam students gain entrance into elite universities.[5]

Given all these advantages, it is not surprising that so many people want to live in Gangnam. People try desperately to maintain their residence or business there even when their financial status is unstable. Older parents living in Gangnam complain that it would make more sense for them to move to a more moderately priced apartment elsewhere. However, they are bound to remain in Gangnam for the sake of their children, since a Gangnam address means a lot in the marital market. Business owners are just as keen to maintain an office in Gangnam for the image it gives the business. Even if the company can barely afford to pay the high rent, relocating would create the impression that the business is failing. In short, Gangnam has become a status symbol. Not surprisingly, Gangnam parents want their children to continue to live in Gangnam after marriage. They want their children to marry spouses who are currently living in Gangnam or are very likely to live there after marriage. On the other side, many non-Gangnam people regret not making a decision to move there earlier when it might have been possible. One survey found that 93 out of 117 non-Gangnam respondents said they would want to move to Gangnam if they were able to, although many of them also expressed negative attitudes toward Gangnam's lifestyle and snobbish atmosphere (Lee and Lee 2017).

Sharing a common material base rooted in the possession of high-value real estate, Gangnam residents naturally have a strong interest in protecting their property values and are extremely sensitive to any government policy change that could threaten those values. It is thus no surprise that in every general election period, all parties compete with one another to propose urban development policies that suit the interests of homeowners, especially those in such influential areas as Gangnam (Son 2008). In most elections since the 1996 general election, Gangnam residents in its three core districts have consistently voted for the conservative ruling-party candidates. The only exception is the 2016 general election when two districts of Gangnam voted for opposition candidates, while five districts went for the conservative candidates. In the most recent 2020 election when the liberal (leftist) ruling party received a landslide victory nationwide, Apgujeongdong residents nonetheless selected an opposition conservative (and ardently anti–North Korea) candidate.

Gangnam residents are also known for a strong sense of class identity among themselves. Ethnographic studies have found that Gangnam residents are well aware that non-Gangnam people consider them to be luxury-oriented, pretentious, and arrogant. But their own perceptions of Gangnam people are different. They see themselves not as mindlessly pursuing luxury and fashion but instead as caring about quality and having discriminating taste. They feel that Gangnam residents are generally better mannered, gentler, more relaxed, and more rational than most others. Naturally, they feel more comfortable staying within their own circles of Gangnam people and show little desire to mix with non-Gangnam people (Lee and Lee 2017). Such attitudes among Gangnam adults seem to be transmitted to their children. Lee's ethnographic study (2017) found that many Gangnam children hold negative views of non-Gangnam areas as being rough, dirty, countrified, smelly, and somewhat dangerous. They may even be afraid of leaving Gangnam (Lee and Lee 2017). Yang (2018b) confirms the same thing. As she reports, "Gangnam residents described their neighbourhoods as 'quiet,' 'clean' and 'ordered,' and portrayed non-Gangnam neighbourhoods as 'loud,' 'narrow,' 'bustling,' 'chaotic.' From the perspective of Gangnam residents, living in Gangnam meant living in a more 'civilised' space" (Yang 2018b, 13). Naturally, such a sense of cultural superiority among Gangnam residents facilitates the development of class identity among these people.

More substantially, living in Gangnam brings advantages in building the kind of social networks that are very helpful in one's career or business. The concentration of power elites and high-income professionals facilitates networking among these influential and resource-rich people. Living in the same large apartment complex, going to the same church, or sending their children to the same schools, they can easily develop close relationships with one another. Being in different occupations, they recognize the value of and consciously seek close relationships with each other. Of course, this kind of class network can develop across different residential areas, but living in close proximity in Gangnam's affluent neighborhoods certainly facilitates such network building and increases the exclusivity of the new upper middle class based on Gangnam residence. As Bae and Joo (2019, 748) observe, "Gangnam residents' modus vivendi is to minimize social exchange with non-Gangnam residents, while actively strengthening their social networks with insiders through school ties or professional affiliations."

Gangnam as a Model of Success

By the early 2000s Gangnam had established itself as a sort of model district, possessing many good things that are desired by urban residents: superior infrastructure, good schools, a modern and global living environment, and most of all the continuous appreciation of real estate values. Gangnam has thus become an object of envy and jealousy for most Koreans. As Gangnam's real estate prices continue to soar, the area has become less and less accessible to other middle-class people. Yet the desire to live in a city like Gangnam is strong, which has fostered a new trend of urban development: to create new cities in the image of Gangnam. Several satellite cities around Seoul, including Bundang, Ilsan, Suseo, and Pyongchon, have been developed on the Gangnam model, and regional cities have created Gangnam-like districts, such as Haewoondae in Busan and Soosung in Daegu. All these new urban spaces are surrounded by upscale shopping centers, good schools and private institutes, renowned hospitals, rows of boutique shops, fashionable restaurants and bars, and trendy leisure places. Park (2017) defines this process as "Gangnam-ization," a process fueled by the desire for Gangnam-style urban space. As he argues, "Gangnam style ... does not remain as a unique feature confined to the area of Gangnam but has become an ideal and dream of urban life that all Korean middle-class people dream and aspire to and is being followed and replicated by every city in Korea" (7).

These newly built towns have obtained moderate success in catching up with the luxury and prestige of Gangnam. But they do not have the same scale of economy that Gangnam possesses, so the size and quality of most facilities, including apartments, shopping areas, and educational facilities, are all one notch lower than Gangnam's. Most critically, their real estate prices have not increased as fast as Gangnam's. The residents of the new luxury towns also seem to experience a sense of relative deprivation vis-à-vis Gangnam residents, knowing that they live in a "lesser Gangnam" because they could not afford to live in the "real Gangnam" (Chang 2017). Hence, while they may be trying hard to distance themselves from ordinary middle-class people, they still have to struggle not to slide too far behind Gangnam residents.

Thus, whether one likes it or not, Gangnam is now accepted as a model of success in many senses. This is not because people admire or respect what Gangnam is about. Much of the popular discourse about Gangnam is still about the speculative real estate investments and conspicuous consumption behaviors of its residents. The media constantly pays attention to the fashionable lifestyles and expensive educational practices among Gangnam's affluent families, making non-Gangnam people envious and jealous of them. No wonder most people desire to live in Gangnam and wish to provide the same kind of educational advantages available to Gangnam children and to develop social ties with socially successful people living in this area. With the rising price of Gangnam apartments, however, it has become almost impossible for ordinary people to move into this area. That raised the practical and symbolic value of having an ownership residence in Gangnam. Thus, Gangnam versus non-Gangnam residence is often used to distinguish the affluent and the ordinary middle classes, except for a few rich neighborhoods in Gangbuk.

Consolidating Class Privilege in the Global Era

It is not an exaggeration to say that Gangnam is the cradle of Korea's privileged upper middle class. But given the origin of its birth, this class has continuously suffered from a sense of its moral illegitimacy. Its political and social power has grown over the years, but mainstream society still looks at Gangnam and its dominant class with a critical eye, although not without envy. The liberal intellectuals who reside in Gangnam are apt to be labeled "Gangnam leftists," pointing to the fact that they may be avowedly progressive but are deeply interested in maintaining their wealth and social privileges. In recent years numerous political scandals have involved the so-called Gangnam leftists, the most prominent of which was the case of Cho Kuk, former presidential aide and former justice minister (for more, see chapter 5). Nonetheless, important changes have occurred in recent decades that have contributed to enhancing the social prestige of Gangnam's upper middle class, so we need to examine the implications of this structural change.

First of all, we must recognize that Gangnam's upper middle class is composed of two distinguishable groups. One group represents the new rich who have accumulated wealth primarily on the basis of real estate investments; some of them are now owners of other businesses, but their primary source of wealth remains the ownership of real estate and rental properties in the Gangnam area. They are the "big hands" in the financial world, the most courted customers of private banks, foreign car dealers, luxury boutique shops, beauty parlors, and the like. The other, a newer group, consists of professional and technical workers employed in the advanced sectors of Korea's globalized economy. Some possess scarce professional skills demanded by the high-tech industries and transnational firms; others possess professional skills (medical, legal, or financial) to serve a rich clientele. Top-ranking state officials can be considered part of this second category.

In the early years of Gangnam's development, it was the first group, the petite bourgeoisie, that was most prominent in Gangnam society and played an influential role in shaping the social and cultural atmosphere of the district. But since the 1990s with the Korean economy's march into globalization, the latter group, professional and technical workers, has become a more important part of Gangnam's upper middle class. These two groups reveal interesting differences in terms of their residential areas as well as their lifestyles. If the first group is more consumerist and seeks to claim their status on the basis of their affluent lifestyle, the latter group is more conservative in their consumption habits and more intent on their children's education. Interestingly, they also tend to be concentrated in different neighborhoods within Gangnam. In general, those with property-based wealth live in Apgujeongdong, where luxury department stores and fancy shops are congregated, while the professional and managerial families are more likely to be found in Daechidong, which is famous as an educational district (Ji 2017). Despite these differences, they do not really constitute two separate classes. In fact, they are often from the same families, with the parental generation more likely to belong to the petite bourgeoisie while their children represent the professional and managerial class. Thus, after one generation of change, Gangnam's affluent class has evolved from what Koreans used to call the *jolbu* (vulgar rich) to what could be called the meritocratic elite or the global middle class, whose members possess high levels of professional and technical skills and global cultural capital. The rise of the latter group within the Gangnam population means greater prestige and cultural legitimacy that can be claimed by Gangnam's upper middle class.

Along with this generational and occupational shift of the Gangnam upper middle class, there are two larger forces that support the legitimacy and privilege of the Gangnam-style upper middle class. One is neoliberalism, which has been established as a major ideology and policy direction in Korea since the 1997–1999 Asian financial crisis. The essence of neoliberalism is in its belief in market principle as a supreme value to be followed in all economic, social, and cultural activities. This belief validates profit-seeking activities and accords high status to those who are alert, flexible, mobile, and skillful in taking advantage of market opportunities. Moreover, the belief justifies people's right to spend their money any way they want to and can protect the rich from public charges of overconsumption. Being rich is now considered to be a beautiful thing, something everybody must strive to become. Thus, the rise of neoliberalism as a powerful ideology in Korea has done much to establish the social status of Gangnam's affluent middle class.

Another factor that has had a powerful effect on Gangnam culture and its reception in Korean society is the rapid globalization of the Korean economy since the mid-1990s. As global culture and global institutional practices gained higher status among Koreans, antipathy toward the American-style consumption practices of affluent Gangnamnites weakened. Gangnam residents are, on average, far more globally mobile and globally connected than other Koreans. They travel abroad frequently, and many of their children study abroad. Their reference group used to be the ordinary American middle class but has now changed to the upper middle class in advanced Western societies. With the deepening globalization of Korean society, Gangnam culture has gained more prestige and legitimacy by embracing globalism and cosmopolitanism.

Given these recent shifts, the new generation of Gangnam's upper middle class represents a sufficiently different group from their parents' generation. Members of the upper middle class possess a far superior level of educational, occupational, and cultural credentials than their parents. They are relatively free of the past image of the Gangnam rich as those who accumulated wealth primarily through speculative real estate investments. Instead, they can claim their status in terms of meritocratic values. Meritocracy is an ideology that justifies bestowing privilege and prestige on those who possess a high level of knowledge and skills and contribute more to production and profit making. Naturally, this ideology is consonant with the interests of those who hold high educational credentials and is therefore gladly embraced by Gangnam's highly educated class. Many of them have attended elite universities in Korea or abroad, speak English well, and have acquired a high level of global and cosmopolitan cultural skills and experiences. If they become successful occupationally and financially, they can easily justify their success on the basis of meritocracy, for they possess enough market merit to claim elite status. As a consequence, it will become increasingly difficult for other people to challenge the new educational elite's claims to social privilege. In this manner, the class privilege enjoyed by Gangnam's upper middle class is becoming slowly consolidated both culturally and ideologically.

5
EDUCATIONAL CLASS STRUGGLE

In October 2019, Korea was roiling over the appointment of Cho Kuk, a prominent leftist political leader, as minister of justice. Huge demonstrations, split between anti-Cho and pro-Cho camps, took place in Seoul almost every other day, each mobilizing tens of thousands of enthusiastic supporters. At the heart of this political controversy were ethical issues concerning the Cho family. In September, the Korean media had reported that Cho's twenty-eight-year-old daughter had allegedly received several unusual benefits from colleges despite her poor school records and had been admitted to a prestigious medical school on the basis of her impressive off-school academic activities, some of which were allegedly falsified. One of the most serious revelations was that she was listed as the first author of an academic article (with a professor and advanced researchers as junior authors) published in a recognized medical journal while she was still in high school. She reportedly had only completed a two-week internship at the lab where the research in question was conducted, and the professor who led the research was a friend of Cho's mother, who was also a professor. It turned out that her mother had arranged several such special opportunities, mobilizing the family's powerful networks and even producing a falsified prize for her daughter from the president of the university where she taught and where her daughter had completed another short-term internship. Continuous revelations about this educational scandal provided powerful ammunition for the critics and political enemies of Cho Kuk, who was himself the most outspoken critic of the conservatives and at the time perhaps the most powerful and trusted political aide of President Moon Jae In. Despite mounting criticism, Moon went ahead with the appointment of Cho as the minister of justice; Cho lasted only three months before resigning to face several criminal charges.

The Cho family scandal was reminiscent of the 2017 scandal that had brought down President Park Geun-hye, whose closest confidante, Choi Sun Sil, exercised illegitimate power to pressure a prestigious women's university to change its admission criteria to admit her daughter. When the story was revealed, the university's students organized a public protest to demand the expulsion of Choi's daughter and a thorough investigation of the university's admission procedures. This small and fairly innocuous protest provided the initial momentum for a series of political demonstrations that eventually led to Park Geun-hye's impeachment.

Anxiety over Education

These events suggest just how important education is in Korean society. No other social issue arouses the intense reactions from the general public that educational issues do, especially when they involve unfair advantages to people of power and wealth. Korean parents have exceptionally high aspirations for their children's education and are willing to invest heavily, even at great sacrifice to themselves, to provide the best education possible for them. The word *kyoyuk'yul*, translated as "education fever" or "education zeal," describes this phenomenon and is pervasive in the discussion of education in Korea. While many Koreans believe that education fever is somewhat unique to Korea (Seth 2002; Lee 2005),[1] they are not, of course, the only people in the world to take a zealous approach to education. In Asia the Chinese, Japanese, and Vietnamese all demonstrate similar levels of educational zeal that may well be due to their shared Confucian cultural tradition. Outside Asia, however, Jews, Nigerians, and many other national, ethnic, and religious communities are famous for similar attitudes.

What seems unique about Korea's educational zeal is not simply the high level of aspiration but rather its combination with a strong egalitarian orientation toward social status and a strong desire for upward social mobility, both of which are the product of Korea's turbulent modern history, including thirty-six years of Japanese colonial rule, the national division between the communist north and capitalist south, and the horrendous Korean War (1950–1953), with its ensuing devastation and widespread poverty. These historical events destroyed the old status system and the ruling class (*yangban*) and ushered in a practically classless society. In this new society, status claims from the old days carried little weight, and people looked on each other as social equals. It was this highly fluid and mobile social structure that established egalitarianism as a key social ethos in Korea, leaving Koreans with little respect for inherited wealth or privilege and a strong belief in equal opportunity and the possibility of upward social mobility through one's own efforts.

The egalitarian spirit among Koreans grew stronger as rapid economic development allowed many people to move up into the middle class. By the late 1970s, as described in chapter 1, about two-fifths of the population could be classified by occupation as middle class, but almost two-thirds of the urban population self-identified as such. Having solved their daily economic problems and acquired a modest amount of economic leeway, many parents wanted to invest their newly acquired resources in their children's education. In fact, whether or not one was able to provide higher education to one's children was often taken as a criterion for middle-class membership. The government facilitated these aspirations by rapidly expanding the public education system. Thus, Koreans' exceptionally strong educational interest is not a simple product of the Confucian value system but instead was fostered by Korea's modern historical experiences, which destroyed the traditional stratification system and opened the door to social mobility for the masses.

Given their strong egalitarian orientation, Koreans are extremely sensitive to issues of equal opportunity and fair play in educational processes. They like to see education as being open to everybody and educational competition as being conducted according to fair rules. When these expectations are violated, especially by those of wealth and power, Koreans react strongly, as demonstrated by the political fallout of the Cho Kuk and Park Geun-hye scandals. The intensity of the public reaction in these cases was directly connected to the widespread perception that education in Korea is becoming more unequal and unfair while also becoming more expensive and stressful. There is a consensus among all sectors of society today that education has ceased to work as a channel of social mobility and now serves instead as a means of class inheritance. For a brief period in the 1960s and 1970s, education was genuinely effective as a social ladder in Korea. The expansion of the secondary schools and universities gave ambitious and talented youngsters from humble backgrounds a realistic chance to climb to the top of the social heap. A large proportion of elite university students in the 1960s and 1970s were from rural farm families or the urban working class. A popular saying at the time was "a dragon from the brook," meaning a person from a humble family background who had achieved an elite position, the Korean version of the American dream. Today, it is more common to hear the lament "no more dragons from the brook."

One interesting puzzle is the discrepancy between outsiders' images of the Korean educational system and the way it is seen by Koreans themselves. From the outside, South Korea seems to have one of the best-performing educational systems in the world. Korean pupils have been performing at the top in standard international tests, often attracting international media attention.[2] And the general educational level in Korea is exceptionally high even compared to other advanced industrial societies; more than 90 percent of middle school students advance to high school, and about 80 percent of them advance to college (including vocational colleges). According to these figures, Korea's population may currently be the most highly educated in the world.

So, South Koreans ought to be proud of their educational achievement. They are, however, extremely dissatisfied with their educational system. Social surveys in Korea often report that education follows only employment problems as the most serious social concern of Korean parents.[3] This discontent is particularly strong among middle-class parents and is one of the main reasons many middle-class people desire to immigrate to the United States, Canada, or Australia.

Why, then, are Koreans so dissatisfied with an educational system that seems to be performing so well from an outside point of view? There are many reasons, but the crux of the matter is that the Korean educational system is too competitive, stressful, and expensive and has only grown worse in all of these ways as South Korea has become an advanced, globalized economy. Why has Korea come to have such an educational system? This is the question I explore in this chapter. In the analysis presented here, I pay close attention to the ways class interest, particularly that of the affluent middle class, has shaped the educational process, often in opposition to the intention of the state's educational policies. Equally important are the roles of neoliberalism and globalization in shaping the educational environment in Korea. My analysis will highlight how growing class inequality in Korea has led to the intensification of educational competition, how the state's efforts to develop a more egalitarian school system were stifled by the class interest of the well-to-do and the rising ideology of neoliberalism, and how this led to the abnormal growth of the private education market. The consequences of these changes have been to make Korea's education increasingly competitive, private-market dependent, and costly in terms of money, time, and information and therefore more closely associated with families' class resources.

The High School Equalization Policy

In principle, a strong desire for education should be a good thing for both individuals and society. Indeed, South Korea's remarkable economic achievement in the past half century owes a lot to the people's educational zeal, which helped to produce a highly educated and disciplined workforce. But educational zeal can become a serious social problem when the rich try to use their money to gain unfair educational advantages for their children, and this is what happened in South Korea as people's living standards improved and the size of the middle class began to grow in the late 1960s. High school enrollment rates increased greatly, and the struggle to enter an elite high school, with an eye to later entering an elite university, intensified as well. Well-to-do families began to use private tutors in order to give a competitive edge to their children. Many of these tutors were moonlighting high school teachers with an excellent track record of improving their students' scores on the college entrance exams. Started by the wealthiest, the practice of hiring expensive tutorial services spread to other middle-class families.

Recognizing the potential danger of this development for the military government, President Park Chung Hee decided to take a drastic measure. A strong believer in egalitarian education and social harmony, he announced the Middle School Equalization Policy in 1969. The policy first abolished the entrance exam for middle schools, replacing it with a random selection procedure based on students' area of residence. Teachers were also reassigned to different schools to promote balance across school districts. Thus, differentials among the middle schools disappeared almost overnight, and so did the need for tutorial education. But, of course, middle school equalization only delayed the competition until it was time for high school entrance exams. Four years later, the government implemented the High School Equalization Policy (HSEP). Again, this policy effectively destroyed the high school ranking system by forcing schools to select their students by using a random selection process rather than entrance exams (Park 2010).

This novel experiment with high school equalization, a rare case in the world, achieved some positive results by ameliorating the exam hell at elementary and middle school levels and reducing the hierarchy among high schools. The policy helped students from poor families receive the same education as those from wealthy families, thus giving a sense of equal opportunity to the mass of the population. But at the same time, the policy produced a serious unintended consequence by promoting a private education market that undermined the public school system. This is because affluent families were ready to explore any possible method to give a competitive edge to their children in the college entrance exams. Their willingness to pay for an educational advantage prompted the rampant growth of the private education market, including cram schools (*hagwons*), tutorial lessons, and an array of private institutes. Despite the government's strenuous efforts to curb the expansion of such private supplementary education, including a policy that ruled private tutoring illegal, demand continued to increase. Public schools were gradually abandoned by well-to-do families, and students gave more serious attention to their off-school education (at *hagwons*), which they believed was doing a better job of preparing them for college entrance exams.

The fundamental flaw in the HSEP was that while it abolished the ranking among high schools, it could not do the same with colleges. Korean universities are notoriously stratified, with a steep hierarchy of prestige in which the top tier is occupied by three universities: Seoul National University, Korea University, and Yonsei University (popularly called the SKY universities). Over the past six decades since Korea's liberation from colonial rule, this school hierarchy has remained basically the same with only minor changes.[4] The graduates of these schools, especially Seoul National University, occupy elite positions in all sectors of Korean society and form tight networks based on school cliques, or *hakbol*. These *hakbol* networks dominate Korean bureaucracies and large corporations (S. Kim 2004). Thus, graduation from one of the elite universities accords lifelong privileges and advantages, both material and symbolic. It is no wonder, then, that Korean middle-class parents are so anxious to have their children attend an elite university and join one of these powerful *hakbol* networks. Korean parents' educational fever is therefore not just a general desire to see their children perform well at school but is also a specific desire to have their children attend one of the elite universities. As long as the university hierarchy remains intact, competition is bound to occur, and resource-rich parents will continue to employ every possible means to help their children acquire an edge in this competition. The main reason the HSEP failed was that the state underestimated the power of class interests. The rise and fall of the HSEP can thus be seen as a battle between the state and class power, which the state lost. This incident also demonstrates how a well-intended policy can produce more problems than it solves when confronted by a powerful class interest.

The Restratification of High Schools

What assisted class power over the state was economic change in the 1980s, specifically the transition of the South Korean economy from labor-intensive, light manufacturing industries to more capital- and knowledge-intensive industries. With this economic transition and under pressure from the United States and other advanced economies, the Chun Doo Hwan government (1980–1987) adopted liberalization as its new policy orientation, although it still maintained a substantial amount of financial and trade regulation. The 1980s–1990s was also a period of broader liberalization that extended beyond the economy. Chun's authoritarian government fell after a mass uprising in 1987, opening the door for political democratization. In the following year, South Korea staged the 1988 Seoul Olympic Games, which helped to promote a liberal social and cultural atmosphere. In the 1990s, neoliberalism became more influential in economic policy and began to spill over into other sectors. Policymakers in the economic branch, which occupied the highest position within the government bureaucracy, strongly advocated the abolition of the HSEP and stressed the need for more flexibility, creativity, and competition in the school system in order to produce the kind of workforce needed for the postindustrial and globalized economy.

It is this changing economic and social environment that led to the reappearance of a high school hierarchy and a restratification of the secondary school system. This restratification occurred in two ways. First, high-ranking public schools emerged in Gangnam's affluent middle-class districts. Second, a new special category of schools was allowed by the state to operate outside the HSEP framework. The first pattern of change was closely related to the increasing residential segregation by class, especially between Gangnam and Gangbuk, as described in chapter 4. Starting from the late 1970s, several of the old elite high schools began to relocate to the predominantly middle-class neighborhoods in Gangnam. This school relocation was part of the state's deliberate strategy to encourage people to move to the newly developed district and was effective in drawing middle-class families pursuing more competitive education for their children. Having relocated to the middle-class areas of Gangnam, these old elite high schools quickly regained their lost status and became a magnet for competitive students from affluent middle-class families.

But middle-class parents' demand for superior education could not be satisfied by the reemergence of a few prime public schools. Entering the 1990s, a second form of high school stratification emerged through the creation of the new category of "special-purpose high schools" (*teukmokko*). The state claimed that these schools were necessary in order to produce more specialists in foreign affairs, science, and engineering—the elite technical and professional workers Korea needed to advance in the global economy. The special high schools were exempt from HSEP restrictions and were allowed to select their own students and run their own curriculum. This was one way the government tried to respond to growing criticism about the alleged downward leveling effect of the HSEP and to allow room for specialized education without abandoning the basic framework of the HSEP. Once established, it did not take long for the special-purpose schools to become the new elite high schools. Elite high schools in Korea are primarily defined by their success in getting a large number of their graduates admitted to elite universities, and the special schools performed excellently in this regard. Some data on student admission rates to elite universities indicate that in 2013, for example, the difference between public and special-purpose schools was as great as ninefold: the public schools admitted 1.4 percent of their graduates to SKY universities, while special-purpose schools admitted 12 percent (Kim 2014).

The target universities for many of the special private schools include universities in the United States and other advanced countries. A few of the Korean private high schools outperform ordinary American high schools in landing their graduates at American Ivy League universities or other elite universities. In 2007, the *Wall Street Journal* conducted a survey of some seven thousand freshmen at eight highly selective colleges in the United States to find out where they went to high school. Two of the top-performing high schools were located in South Korea: "The 10 schools that performed best in our survey are all private schools. Two top performers overall are located in South Korea. Daewon Foreign Language High School in Seoul sent 14 percent of its graduating class to the eight colleges we examined. That's more than four times the acceptance rate of the prestigious Horace Greeley High School in Chappaqua, N.Y." (*Wall Street Journal*, November 30, 2007).[5]

Not surprisingly, the student bodies at special-purpose and autonomous (*jasako*) schools are predominantly composed of students from the middle and upper-middle class. The tuition rates alone would probably ensure this, but because entrance is so competitive, many of the students had to attend competitive cram schools in Gangnam beforehand. Although the special-purpose schools were intended to produce specialists in science, engineering, and foreign languages, many of their students, once they enter the universities, change their majors to business management, law, or other popular fields.

The Expansion of the Private Education Market

The restratification of the high schools brought the predictable consequence of intensifying educational competition. When the HSEP was in full force, school competition occurred at the senior level of high school, but now it spread down to the middle school and elementary school levels and even lower. Parents relied more and more on cram schools and private tutoring to prepare their children to apply to selective private high schools. Thus, the private education market began to expand even more vigorously, producing a huge education industry that overpowered and outperformed the regular schools. The rate of *hagwon* growth has been especially fast since the early 2000s, as shown in figure 5.1. This change was related to the lifting in 2000 of a legal restriction that had been

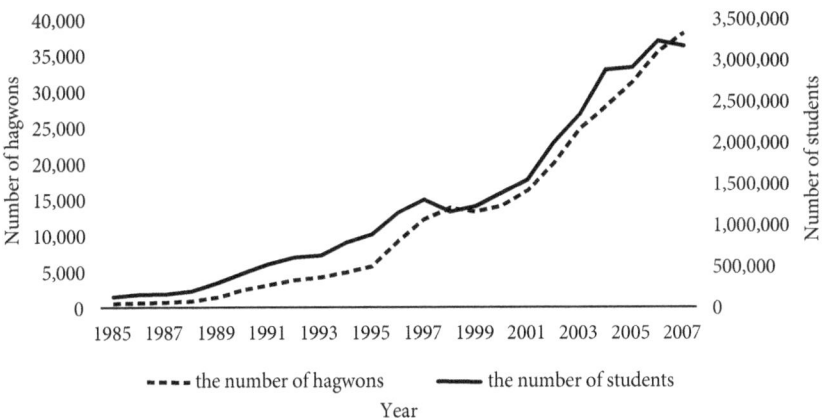

FIGURE 5.1. Number of *hagwon*s and students, 1985–2007

Source: Song (2008).

placed on cram schools and tutorial activities and to a growing demand for English education since the Asian financial crisis.

This rapid expansion of private after-school education led to the equally fast increase of educational expenses for individual families. In 1990 Korean families spent an average of 8.2 percent of their total household expenses on education. By 2013 this had increased to 11.7 percent. As a nation, in the early 2000s Korea was spending the largest proportion of gross national product (2.79%) for private education among the OECD economies (Kim 2010).[6] In 2003, for instance, Korea's expenditure on private education amounted to US$12.4 billion, which was equivalent to about 56 percent of the national budget on education (Lee 2005).

Virtually all families above the poverty level participate in supplementary private education. Not surprisingly, the extent and form of that participation varies according to family income levels. In 2005, households in the top 10 percent income bracket spent a monthly average of 292,000 won (US$286) on private education, which was eight times as much as the 36,000 won (US$35) spent by the bottom 10 percent (*Korea Times*, August 8, 2005).

Many *hagwon*s have become large and prosperous business organizations. They are able to recruit talented teachers and provide education perfectly tailored to preparing for college admission tests. Interestingly enough, many of the star *hagwon* teachers and successful entrepreneurs in the private education industry were involved in the antigovernment democracy movement of the 1980s. Most of them graduated from, or dropped out of, elite universities. But because of their history of political activism, and in some cases prison records, they were barred from entering the corporate sector or government bureaucracy. Obtaining work in the shadow education market was one of the few options open to them, and their early training in political debate and argumentation from their student activist days is an advantage in this field. These skills prove very useful in teaching students how to prepare for the essay tests that only recently became an important part of the college admission procedure. It is ironic that those who were once at the vanguard of the struggle for democracy became the main contributors to the expansion of the private education industry, thereby helping to make Korean education more unequal and class-determined.

What is particularly troubling about the development of Korea's private education industry is its uneven spatial distribution between Seoul and the countryside and between Gangnam and Gangbuk in Seoul. Gangnam occupies a very important place in this development. We have seen how Gangnam emerged as a prime residential location where first-rate schools and private institutions are concentrated. One particular neighborhood in Gangnam, Daechidong, is known as the mecca of Korean private education; it is considered to have the nation's most competitive *hagwon*s with the best teachers and the most advanced teaching methods. With their excellent records of getting their students into elite universities, these top *hagwon*s are themselves so competitive that students will sometimes attend other *hagwon*s to prepare for admittance to their preferred *hagwon*. Unlike in other areas, the *hagwon*s in Daechidong tend to be small and provide specialized and customized lessons. Housing prices in Daechidong are high even by the Gangnam standard, so few but the very wealthy can move there permanently. Nevertheless, many temporary residents rent apartments to access the educational facilities in this area. During the summertime, Daechidong draws students from other areas who are eager to take special courses from well-known *hagwon* teachers.

Gangnam Moms

When it comes to private education in Korea, a subject that has drawn a great deal of attention in both the media and scholarly discussion is the so-called Gangnam moms (E. Kim 2004; Kim 2006; Park 2007; SBS 2007). They figure prominently whenever people talk about Korea's education fever or the problems of the overblown private education market. The media and popular literature treat Gangnam moms as either heroes or villains of the Gangnam style of education—an aggressive and highly materialistic approach geared to providing the maximum advantage to one's own children by investing heavily in private education. According to the popular discourses on these mothers, nothing is more important to them than their children's education. Gangnam moms firmly believe that education is the only sure channel for success in Korea, which means that their children must attend elite universities in order to inherit parents' social status. Gangnam moms also believe that Korea's public school system is almost defunct and that they must seek a more effective way to provide an educational edge to their children through the private off-school market. Therefore, Gangnam moms are willing—and more able than most—to invest heavily in all varieties of private education that have congregated in Gangnam.

But what distinguishes Gangnam moms from other middle-class mothers is not their educational zeal and willingness to pay for private supplementary education but rather their whole approach to educating their children. Both scholars and popular writers often characterize Gangnam moms as "education managers." In fact, a few Gangnam moms I interviewed liked to describe themselves as such. As the label suggests, they do not see their role as merely supportive; they are not satisfied with giving their children access to private education and encouraging them to work hard. Rather, they understand the private education market as almost a jungle, inhabited by an exuberant overgrowth of diverse educational services of differing qualities. Therefore, their job is to cut a path for their children: to find the best cram schools, arrange the most competent teachers and counselors, and devise the most effective strategies to prepare for the ever-changing college admission policies. Meeting these challenges requires more than money and zeal. It requires first-rate information, intelligent assessment of options, and skillful planning and strategizing. Gangnam moms are keenly aware of this fact, which is why they see the need to actively manage their children's educational careers.

Becoming an effective education manager is not easy. It presupposes a high level of educational competence on the part of the mother as well as the financial resources to implement what she determines to be the best strategies. In addition, access to high-quality information is crucial. Gangnam moms are therefore famous for their industriousness. The ideal Gangnam mom never misses the public seminars on college admission held by the large cram schools; she visits bookstores and studies informational materials carefully and keeps a close eye on the nation's constantly changing university admissions system, assiduously collecting admission-related information. But the most important sources of information are other experienced and well-connected mothers, which leads Gangnam moms to form small networks in which they share information and organize socializing activities for their children. The goal of most of the mothers is to join the networks of mothers with the best-performing children, superior information, or both, while the mothers of the top students want to stick together and exclude the mothers of mediocre students. Women employed outside the home, even if they are highly educated professionals, are unwelcome in these networks because they will not be able to contribute as much as the full-time education manager mothers.

In addition to their managerial role, Gangnam moms are popularly known as having a certain attitude. In the popular perception, Gangnam moms are people with a highly materialistic and instrumental orientation to education. They look at education primarily as a means of success. They care little about the content of high school education, as they are really only concerned with whether or not a school is preparing their children effectively for the college entrance exams. In that regard, Gangnam moms have withdrawn their trust from public schools and given it to well-reputed *hagwons*, tutors, and counselors. These parents' strong trust in the power of superior supplementary education seems to encourage their highly materialistic orientation to education. Many of them seem to believe that educational success can be purchased with money. Some mothers are optimistic that even a mediocre student can be made a success—that is, gain admission to an elite university—if properly taught and coached by private teachers and counselors. This, of course, requires a substantial financial investment. And like any other investment, funds must be invested in the right way to produce optimum return. This is the role of the competent Gangnam mom. Fathers are usually absent from this picture. They are the providers of necessary funds, but the managers—the ones with the pertinent information and the social contacts—are the mothers.

In short, Gangnam has emerged in Korea as the place of greatest privilege in terms of educational opportunities. Gangnam students attend better public and private schools and have access to top-quality cram schools and tutorial services. Moreover, many of them are actively assisted by the highly motivated education managers who are their mothers. Meanwhile, non-Gangnam parents observe Gangnam students' educational advantages with anxiety and frustration. Such a feeling was well expressed by a middle-class mother I interviewed in 2006 in Seoul:

> When it comes to education for our children, we are willing to sacrifice as much as we can. And we are trying to do everything that people around us are doing. But when I hear [through the media] what those rich people in Gangnam are doing, my heart sinks. There is no way we can catch up with them. As far as other things are concerned, like taking an overseas trip, we can at least try to do something similar. Instead of going to America or Europe, we may make a trip to Bangkok or Japan. And we don't care about or envy what they are eating. But when it comes to education, it makes us so frustrated and angry. It makes me feel we are the losers.

The Impact of Neoliberalism

From the 1990s, neoliberal ideologies have driven the transformation of the Korean educational system. First introduced in the 1980s during the Chun Doo Hwan government, neoliberalism gained dominance in Korea after the Asian financial crisis. Since then, the Korean educational system has undergone many important changes under the powerful influence of neoliberal ideologies.

The first major effect of neoliberalism on education was that it provided the ideological support for liberalizing education in opposition to the HSEP. We have already seen the appearance of special-purpose high schools (*teukmokko*) in the 1990s. These special schools were allowed to operate outside the purview of HSEP regulations. But in the early 2000s, the Kim Dae Jung government allowed another form of independent schools, autonomous private high schools (*jasakos*). For Kim's liberal and left-leaning government, it was not easy to introduce this kind of exception to the ideal of equal education, but the changing ideological environment empowered neoliberal-minded educators to persuade the state to implement this policy. During the ensuing conservative government of Lee Myung Bak (2008–2013), the number of *jasakos* increased further. Special-purpose schools and autonomous private schools share many common features: they are almost all private, their tuition is high, their teaching staff is better qualified, and their curricula have a strong international orientation. Consequently, they are far more successful than other schools in getting their graduates admitted to elite universities.

In 2000, the ascending ideology of neoliberalism produced a somewhat surprising event in the judiciary branch of the government. In the winter of that year, the Constitutional Court ruled that the state's ban on tutorial education was unconstitutional. This is the ban the Chun Doo Hwan government had imposed in order to curb the private off-school education industry, which had grown in reaction to the HSEP. Liberal educators had long pointed out the illegality of the ban, and wealthy parents had continuously tried to evade it, but successive governments felt obligated to enforce the ruling. But now, supported by the rising power of neoliberalism, liberal educators and affluent families were able to influence the Constitutional Court to rule against the state restriction on private education. By removing the ban, the higher court opened the door for all kinds of private moneymaking educational services, and the number of cram schools, private institutes, tutoring services, educational consultants, and the like exploded.

Entering the twenty-first century, neoliberalism's continuing dominance brought deeper ideological consequences for Korean education not just on the structural and organizational level but also in educational philosophy and the daily conduct of educational practices. The old progressive ideology of educational equality and state control of education lost its appeal to educators. Instead, the neoliberal values of competition, performance, flexibility, and freedom of choice were taken as guiding principles of educational reform. Increasingly, emphasis is placed on self-development and individual responsibility and on the necessity of measuring skills and performance with objective and quantifiable measures.

This neoliberal trend introduced an important change in the ways Korean college students try to prepare themselves for employment. A neologism that became popular in the mid-2000s and is talked about constantly among college students is "specs," which comes from "specifications," the detailed list of features included in electronic and other consumer products. For students, specs are basically academic credentials and experiences. In the escalating competition for a small number of good jobs in the corporate sector and state bureaucracy, students came to believe that their chances of employment depend heavily on the quantity and quality of the specs they can present on their résumés. Obviously, the more impressive their specs the better their chances, so millennials are deeply concerned with building their résumés. Many take a year off from school just to improve their specs, a practice that is especially common among first-tier university students. As Hae-joang Cho, an anthropology professor at Yonsei University, observes, "Upon entering a prestigious college with a lucrative major, students continue studying for the English Proficiency Test, aim for a high grade point average (GPA), prepare for various contests and qualification tests, and participate in study-abroad and internship programs.... These young people whose lives are centered on accumulating specs cannot stand to waste time. My students said they have been practicing time management from early childhood. I learned that neoliberal manuals of self-development were among the favorite readings of these students" (Cho 2015, 446). Cho's description suggests how deeply neoliberal ideologies have penetrated into the inner life of Korean students. Today's students are so preoccupied with building their specs that they are losing interest in and actually find no time for reading interesting books or engaging in culturally and socially meaningful activities.

Another important change brought by the neoliberal shift of educational policy in recent years is the adoption of a new college admissions procedure modeled after one practiced in the United States. In the past, Korean universities admitted students in one fixed period of selection based on the Scholastic Aptitude Test, high school GPA, and a university-specific test. But in the new neoliberal environment, Korean universities began to stress new qualification criteria such as creativity, diversity, flexibility, and self-learning capacity. Test forms also changed, giving more weight to essay tests designed to evaluate students' ability to demonstrate active knowledge by presenting ideas and logical arguments rather than passive, memorized knowledge. At the same time, many Korean universities, especially the top-tier ones, adopted a multistep selection procedure, which expanded the process beyond a fixed selection period. In this procedure, first-tier applicants are selected through an American-style advanced admission procedure, ahead of students who are selected through the regular competition process. Most high-performing students hope for advanced admission, for which they need to present exceptional specs. This is why ambitious students struggle to accumulate high English test scores, internships, awards from various contests, certificates, voluntary work, paper presentations, adventurous overseas travel experience, and the like (Abelmann, Park, and Kim 2009). But as revealed by the aforementioned case of Cho Kuk's daughter, outstanding specs are often constructed with the active help of resourceful parents who can mobilize assistance from a wide network of friends, colleagues, and specialists in various fields. A simple unpaid internship at some research organization may be easy to arrange for professional parents but is almost unobtainable for most lower-class students. Therefore, as the college admission procedures become more complicated and neoliberal in intent, ordinary middle-class children experience more disadvantages in competition with children from professional and managerial families.

In sum, many changes have occurred in Korea's educational system over the past four decades, driven by privatization, globalization, and the rise of neoliberalism. These forces have all worked to make the educational system in Korea more complex and competitive, which in turn has enhanced the power of class resources in determining educational success and failure. Economic capital may have been the main form of class power in the old days. In today's globalized world, class reproduction also requires social and cultural capital (in the form of information and knowledge) because these determine an individual's educational opportunities. Numerous policy changes, despite their good intentions, have ended up being defeated or distorted by class power and class interest. The end result is an educational system that is extremely complex, anxiety-producing, and class-dependent. One of my interviewees articulated the depth of many Korean parents' anxiety and frustration with this situation:

> In the old days, educating a child was a far simpler thing. Parents used to tell children just to study hard, listen to teachers well at school, do homework diligently, and like that. Now, it is so complicated. Now we must send them to private English lessons, math *hagwon*s, piano lessons, essay-preparing *hagwon*s, you name it. But that's not enough. We must worry about whether or when we must send them abroad for study. We hear all kinds of stories about early study abroad, good and bad. . . . We

don't know how much is enough. Like everybody else, we want to give the best education to our children. We want to see them succeed in life. So we try our best, but it's so hard . . . and we don't know whether we are doing enough. [I am afraid] others may be doing more, smarter things than we are doing. I don't know. It's so difficult. Education really is full of pain to me.

Class Reproduction

A popular discourse that appeared in Korea in the 2010s is the familiar spoon theory of class inheritance: some people are born with a silver spoon in their mouth and enjoy a good life thanks to their fortunate origin; others are born with a bronze or even a dirt (earthenware) spoon and lead a dreadful life. This dark characterization of Korean society circulated among young people first through social media and then entered the mainstream media as a popular topic of debate and commentary. Most older adults today are surprised to see such pessimistic attitudes among the young and wonder why young people seem not to understand or care about Korea's accomplishment in creating an affluent society out of abject poverty through tremendous endurance and hard work. But from the standpoint of the young, it is the older generations who cannot understand how dreadful the opportunity structure is today for all but a fortunate few.

What troubles many people today is that Korean society offers few chances for upward social mobility. In the past, the educational system created the possibility for people from farming families and urban working-class backgrounds to move into the respectable middle class. That is why the older generations had such great faith in the educational system and were so eager to provide the best education they could for their children. But today the parental generations no longer see the Korean educational system as functioning in the same way. The system, in their eyes, is not only too costly and stressful but also systematically biased in favor of the rich and against the poor. It is not just the poor who suffer disadvantages but also the majority of middle-class people, who also feel that their children are deprived of equal opportunities to compete with the children of affluent families.

Much of the research on Korea's educational inequality deals with the wide divergence between Gangnam and Gangbuk in terms of children's chances of being admitted to elite universities. One particularly significant study was done by Se-Jik Kim (2014), a professor at Seoul National University (SNU), who used data provided by SNU to analyze the school's differential rates of admission by socioeconomic factors. His analysis found that in 2014, some districts in Gangnam landed their high school graduates at SNU at rates 15–21 times higher than the rates of the least successful districts in Gangbuk. More specifically, in terms of the numbers per 100 students, Gangnam's three core districts (Gangnam-gu, Seocho-gu, and Songpa-gu) recorded 2.1, 1.5, and 0.8 students admitted to SNU, while several districts in Gangbuk had 0.1–0.3 students admitted. Kim's analysis also revealed a remarkable divergence between the special-purpose and autonomous high schools and other public schools in admission rates to SNU. In 2014, only 0.6 out of 100 students graduating from ordinary public schools in Seoul were admitted to SNU, compared to 10 from foreign-language schools and 41 from special-purpose science schools. Kim's data further suggest that this gap widened rapidly between 2005 and 2014.

The most telling data presented in Kim's study show a close correlation between the real estate prices in Gangnam area and the rates of admission to SNU (figure 5.2). His analysis also reveals a high correlation (R = 0.74) between the average apartment price in each neighborhood and the rate of admission to elite universities, offering evidence that wealthier residential areas have a larger number of *hagwons* that can significantly improve students' chances of getting admitted to elite universities.

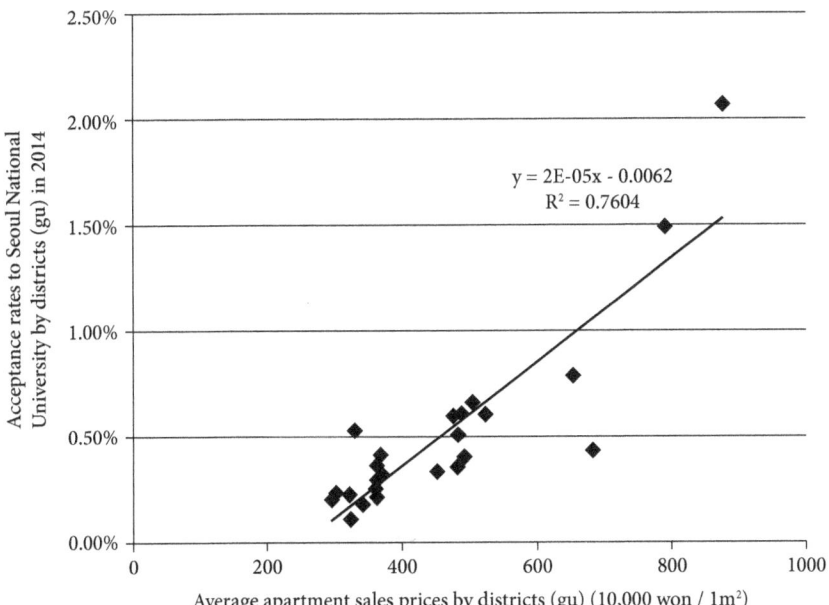

FIGURE 5.2. Apartment prices and acceptance rates to Seoul National University, 2014

Source: Kim (2014).

One sociological study (Y. Kim 2016) investigated whether parents' class effects (measured by education and occupation) on children's chances of attending universities located in Seoul (which are considered more prestigious and more competitive in terms of admittance than universities outside Seoul) vary across different cohorts. The study found that parental effects are significantly stronger among the students in their twenties than those in their thirties, which indicates decreasing chances of social mobility today compared even to a decade ago.

These data can explain why the spoon theory of class finds such resonance with Korean youths: spoon theory reflects the reality they experience daily in the extremely competitive education system and job market. In fact, these data pertain to only half of the educational inequality they confront—that is, the competition for elite universities inside Korea. The other half is the newly developing inequality in access to global education. The class effect is even stronger in the case of overseas education than in domestic education. As we will see in chapter 6, affluent families have far more resources than lower-middle–class families to employ diverse strategies regarding overseas education for their children.

The general trend in Korea is definitely a deepening relationship between class and educational opportunities. In this trend, the social class that plays the most critical role is undoubtedly the affluent middle class who possess adequate economic and cultural resources to adapt to the changing educational market and who takes education most seriously to ensure their children inherit the status of their parents. One important difference between the affluent middle class and the upper class is that while the latter can ensure class reproduction through inheritance of wealth or business ownership, the children of professional and managerial families must participate in the competitive educational process to maintain their parents' status. What we have seen in this chapter is that the affluent middle class has been central in promoting after-school private education, thereby making Korea's educational process more intense, stressful, and financially costly. Yet in the end, everybody is a victim of this extraordinarily competitive education system.

6
IN PURSUIT OF GLOBAL EDUCATION

On January 9, 2005, the *Washington Post* featured an article about a Korean family who had immigrated to the United States. The Kim family, settled in a suburban district of Maryland, was composed of a mother and three young children ages four, eleven, and thirteen. They came not for economic reasons or to reunite with family but instead to pursue a better education. Interestingly, the husband and father of the family did not come with them and stayed in Korea, where he worked to finance the family's overseas stay. As the article describes their situation, "They are called kirogi, or wild geese—South Korean families separated by an ocean. The parents want their children to be taught in the United States, but the cost of an American education can be the fracturing of the family" (Ly 2015). (Wild geese are known among Koreans for their lifelong dedication to their mates and for flying great distances to bring food to their nestlings.) The Kim family seemed to be doing fine: the three children were happy with their new school lives in America, the mother was busy managing the children's education, and the father, a company executive in Korea, kept in close touch through daily long-distance calls and two or three visits a year. Splitting a family across the ocean certainly has its costs emotionally and financially, but "the separation is bearable, [Mrs.] Kim said, when she thinks about the advantages they are giving their children."

On June 8, 2008, a similar article appeared in the *New York Times* titled "For English Studies, Koreans Say Goodbye to Dad" (Onishi 2008). This is a story of *kirogi* families in Auckland, New Zealand, and reports that "South Koreans now make up the largest group of foreign students in the United States (more than

103,000) and the second largest in New Zealand after Chinese students." As the author recognizes, Korea's "wild geese" phenomenon is different from a more traditional pattern of migration because it is the women and children who go overseas rather than the men and also because the principle motivation is educational, not financial. "Driven by a shared dissatisfaction with South Korea's rigid educational system," the author explains, "parents in rapidly expanding numbers are seeking to give their children an edge by helping them become fluent in English, while sparing them, and themselves, the stress of South Korea's notorious educational pressure cooker."

These two newspaper articles represent only a small sample from the tremendous amount of international media attention given to Korea's wild geese families. Split-family educational migration is not unique to Korea, however. In Hong Kong, Taiwan, and China, terms such as "astronauts," "satellite children," and "parachute kids" are used to refer to children who are sent to the United States or Canada for educational purposes and also as a link for subsequent family migration (Ong 1998; Pe-Pua et al. 1998; Chee 2003; Parreñas 2005; Waters 2005; Douglass 2006; Abelmann, Newendorp, and Lee-Chung 2014; Lan 2018). But Korea seems to stand out in terms of the magnitude and intensity of this split-family form of early study abroad. Onishi (2008) estimated the total number of Korean schoolchildren in the United States to be around forty thousand in the early 2000s.

The wild geese families are clearly a product of globalization, and the magnitude of this phenomenon in Korea is related to the aggressive manner in which the state has embraced globalization and stressed the importance of global educational skills. In addition, the painful experience of the Asian financial crisis made Koreans realize the necessity of possessing global skills to survive in the unpredictable economic environment. This chapter describes how globalization has affected the ways affluent middle-class families have adapted to the globalized education market and tried to devise new strategies to give their children a competitive edge in education.

Globalization and the English Craze

The most obvious way globalization has affected the Korean educational process is by making English competence a crucial skill for doing well at school and finding a good job afterward. In Korea, English-language ability had been regarded as a special skill and almost a mark of the elite since the Korean War or even before. But its value has increased greatly since President Kim Young Sam announced his *sekyehwa* (globalization) policy in 1994. One important part of the *sekyehwa* policy included a plan to improve the level of English competence in the general population and, as a specific measure, mandated schools to start teaching English in elementary grades rather than waiting until middle school. This new policy meant more than adding another subject to the elementary school curriculum. It also meant that English would become the most important subject in children's entrance exams for high school. Elementary schools scrambled to find able English teachers, who were in short supply, and the quality of English education came to be taken almost as a proxy measure of a school's quality. Middle-class parents, who were always preoccupied with how to improve their children's competitive edge in college entrance exams, immediately responded by starting their children's English education at a very early age, most often through private tutoring.

What accelerated this trend was the Asian financial crisis that arrived in Korea in 1997. The industrial restructuring that followed was focused on improving Korea's global competitiveness, and all major firms and government organizations began to stress globally competitive skills for their managerial workforces. English competence was an essential and easily observable element of this global competence. At the same time, an important lesson Korean workers took from the financial crisis was the need to possess extra skills in order to survive this kind of huge economic shake-up. English-language ability came to be seen as a tool in one's survival kit for the new harsh world, and this perception prompted many midcareer officials and managerial workers to spend a great deal of their nonwork time trying to improve their English.

Meanwhile, the rapidly globalizing economy after the crisis shifted the job market in favor of highly skilled workers. Many transnational firms came in to establish affiliate firms in Korea and brought lucrative job opportunities for those who were proficient in English. And as Korean conglomerate firms became more globalized in their operations, their demand for a globally skilled workforce increased as well. By the late 1990s, more and more of the big Korean companies were requiring a job interview in English as part of the screening process. Speaking good English became a prerequisite even at many smaller firms, regardless of whether they had a use for it. Thus, English came to be valorized as an essential skill and a measure of competence in the new global age. Those who lacked adequate English-language skills came to be regarded as outdated and lacking the cultural and social aptitude required for the global business environment.

In a short time, the whole society became wrapped up in the frenzy to learn English. This frenzy affected every group—elementary students preparing for entrance exams for select private high schools, high school students preparing for comprehensive scholastic tests, college students preparing for a job or postgraduate education, and many white-collar workers concerned with promotion or job maintenance. It is no surprise that the English frenzy produced a mushrooming market for English-language education, especially because the public schools were slow in meeting the demand. The fact that English-language education, especially of high quality, is conducted outside the formal schools makes it a high-cost expenditure for all families. According to one estimate, the English-language educational market was around 10 trillion won (US$10 billion) per year in the early 2000s. Private English-language institutes made about 2 trillion won; the rest involved study abroad (*Chosun Daily* January 16, 2006). And a *Dong-a Daily* poll in 2006 found that 80 percent of parents with elementary or secondary school children were giving them private English education of some kind, at an average household expenditure of 1.97 million won ($2,016) per year (Donga.com, 3/30/2006).

Early Study Abroad

Soon, middle-class families were not satisfied even with the English-language education available at private institutes. Parents seeking a more effective method of instilling the language in their children realized that it must be taught as early as possible and preferably in a native English-speaking environment. Thus, the late 1990s saw the birth of a new trend of sending young children to English-speaking countries for early study abroad.

Until the late 1980s, very few precollege Korean students went abroad. But the number of children going abroad increased sharply from the late 1990s to the early 2000s. According to the *Korea Times* (January 3, 2006), "The number of elementary students studying overseas has snowballed from 212 in 1998 to 6,276 in 2004, making a 30-fold rise. The number of middle-school students increased from 473 to 5,568 over the same period, while that of high school students jumped from 877 to 4,602." Figure 6.1 shows the rapid increase in the number of early study-abroad students until 2006, when it reached 29,511 and then began to decline. This was an entirely new pattern of study abroad, signaling the new era of globalized education. In the past, Koreans going abroad for study were mainly graduate or postgraduate students. In fact, until the 1980s sending high school children abroad and sending money to children studying abroad were officially disallowed.

The *kirogi* families' main destination is the United States, but other popular destinations include Canada, Australia, New Zealand, and England. Korean schoolchildren even go to countries such as India, the Philippines, Singapore,

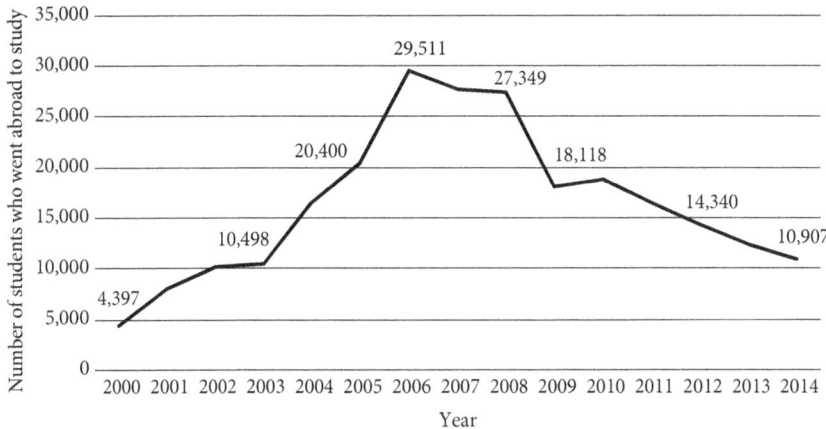

FIGURE 6.1. The trend of early study abroad (number of persons)

Source: Korean Educational Statistics Service (2015).
https://kess.kedi.re.kr/mobile/stats/school?menuCd=0101&cd=5498&survSeq=2021&itemCode=01&menuId=m_010105&uppCd1=010105&uppCd2=010105&flag=A.

and South Africa, where English is used as a standard language for the educated population.

A small number of such split families had existed in Korea before the 1990s. Most of them involved fathers (rarely mothers) assigned to overseas work (such as diplomats and corporate managers) or academics who spent a sabbatical year in America or Europe. When it was time to return home, some of these families decided to leave their children behind so they could continue their education in metropolitan centers. If the child was too young to stay alone, the mother might decide to stay a little longer. In the earlier period, most of these overseas-educated children returned to Korea and were able to enter elite universities through special tracks allowed by the government for children of overseas-stationed diplomats, corporate executives, and other professionals. After the Asian financial crisis, this elite strategy of global education was quickly adopted by other affluent families even if they had no overseas experiences or connections. In the early 2000s, many small business owners and independent property owners also joined the race for early English-language education abroad. By the first decade of the twentieth century, the desire to have their children educated abroad had become ubiquitous among middle-class parents regardless of their economic situation. According to a poll conducted by the *Dong-a Daily* in 2006, one out of four Korean parents said that if the opportunity were available, they would want to emigrate for the sake of their children's education. This inclination was stronger among younger parents. Among parents in their thirties with children in elementary school, 41 percent expressed a willingness to emigrate for the children's education, and 20 percent of fathers said they were willing to become "*kirogi* fathers" (Donga.com, 3/30/2006).

Studies on *kirogi* families found two primary reasons for this form of educational migration (Cho 2005; Lee and Koo 2006; Kim 2011; Finch and Kim 2012; Shin 2014). One is dissatisfaction with the Korean educational system. *Kirogi* parents complain that Korean education is simply too competitive, expensive, and stressful and express their desire to get their children away from Korea's pressure-cooker educational system and allow them to study in a freer and more educationally cultivating environment. The other is, of course, the desire for the children to learn English at an early age and acquire native-like fluency, which the parents believe will confer a huge advantage in the struggle to succeed in the globalized world. Korean parents' discontent with the Korean educational system is well known and well grounded, but it was only after Korea's liberalization and active embrace of globalization that middle-class families had the freedom to send their kids abroad. This is undoubtedly an extremely expensive project even for most middle-class families. In 2014, paying for private school tuition and living expenses for a child and mother in the United States, excluding expenses for extracurricular activities, required almost 100 million won (US$94,000) a year (Lee 2014). But after the shock of the Asian financial crisis, many white-collar and managerial workers became convinced that survival in today's competitive environment requires extra market credentials, among which English fluency is primary. Many of them say that sending their children for study abroad is the best investment they could make toward giving them a brighter and more secure future.

Confucian *Kirogi* Families?

Seeing so many Korean families take such a drastic step, foreigners often wonder how this is possible in a Confucian society. On the face of it, *kirogi* families seem counter to the ideal model of the Confucian family, which prioritizes family solidarity and togetherness. As Onishi (2008) writes, "living apart for years strains marriages and undermines the role of a father, traditionally the center of the family in South Korea's Confucian culture." Until recently, the most typical Confucian middle-class families had a father who was expected to work hard in an exacting workplace and return home to be comforted by his caring wife and obedient, well-behaved children. The mother/wife was normally bound to the domestic realm, where she was supposed to take care of the house, the children, and her parents-in-law. The idea of a wife moving to a faraway place with the children while leaving the father/husband alone at home seems completely contrary to this norm.

Yet as several scholars (Chang 1997, 2018; Cho 2005; Lee and Koo 2006; Finch and Kim 2012) have acknowledged, Korea's *kirogi* families do not deviate from the Confucian family norm as they might seem to be at first glance; in fact, they are possible precisely because of the Confucian ideal. As we have seen, the main motivation of *kirogi* parents is to give the best education possible to their children; this is exactly what Confucianism stresses as a prime value. *Kirogi* parents are willing to sacrifice so much—financially, emotionally, and socially—because they are deeply imbued with the Confucian value system that regards education as a chief criterion for social recognition and social achievement. Furthermore, in Confucian thinking, children's education is not an individual matter but rather a collective family project. A child's educational success or failure is taken as a measure of how the family is doing in terms of social honor and respectability. Middle-class families thus may look at early study abroad as a strategic and necessary investment to maintain the family's (upper) middle-class status. Such thinking justifies and encourages parents' willingness to sacrifice because their children's success is their own success and source of happiness.

It is also important to recognize that despite physical separation, *kirogi* families generally maintain traditional gender relations between the mother/wife and the father/husband. The father is the principal breadwinner and financial provider for the overseas family members and enjoys patriarchal authority over them. The father takes on the burden of supporting the family abroad and suffers loneliness by living alone, but making this sacrifice supports his claims to authority and respect. On the other side, the wife/mother performs the hard job of managing the children's education in a strange environment and also suffers the emotional cost of separation from her spouse. So, while being separated, wife and husband continue to perform their traditional duties.

One in-depth interview study of *kirogi* mothers in the United States made the following observation:

> Our study reveals how closely related kirŏgi families are to their counterparts in Korea. Kirŏgi families emphasize family integrity and the continuity with their previous lives in Korea. The wives whom we interviewed stressed their unswerving commitment to the institutions of marriage and the family. Kirŏgi spouses adhere to strict gender roles, with the husband as the breadwinner and the wife as the household— and especially the education—manager. These roles are carried over from Korea, and they are not drastically altered by having a split

household. In fact, many women asserted that their family relations were the same as before or even strengthened by the phenomenon. (Finch and Kim 2012, 502)

Another in-depth interview study focused on *kirogi* fathers remaining in Korea (Lee and Koo 2006) also suggests strong family solidarity and close cooperation among *kirogi* parents, though with a substantial amount of financial and emotional strain. While there is a popular suspicion that it is the mothers who are behind the decision to split the family, *kirogi* fathers also play an active and supportive role in choosing this family adventure:

> Our data suggest that *kirogi* fathers were not passive or reluctant participants in this scheme. To the contrary, they were often the initiators of this family splitting for the sake of children and, despite the great difficulties they have to endure, they seem to have no regret about their decisions. Furthermore, despite long periods of physical separation, our *kirogi* fathers seem to be able to maintain stable and normal relationships with their wives and children. In some cases, the father's guiding role in children's education from a distance increases along with his emotional attachment to the family. (Lee and Koo 2006, 551)

These findings suggest that educationally motivated transnational split families are not necessarily deviating from the Confucian family ideal. Abnormal as they may appear, *kirogi* families reveal a commitment to core cultural values of Confucianism, including respect for education, the family as a unit of collective interest, a strong commitment to marital union, traditional gender relations, and intimate mother-child relationships. As Cho (2005) argues, "The persisting cultural values of familism assists the formation of transnational households as much as structural forces of globalization propel it." But we must also acknowledge that this familism differs from the traditional form in some important aspects. As Lee and Koo (2006, 552) argue, "*kirogi* families reveal strong family solidarity, but this solidarity is based on a more flexible and pragmatic form of family relations than the traditional patriarchal model." This view agrees with several Korean scholars' view of "new familism" in Korea as "instrumental," "adaptive," or "flexible" (Chang 1997; Cho 2005).

The Waning of *Kirogi* Families

As we have seen, *kirogi* families increased rapidly from the late 1990s to the late 2000s. But interestingly enough, their growth came to a sudden halt and began to decline from 2008, as shown in figure 6.1. The main reason for this reversal was obviously the Great Recessions of 2007–2008. During this global economic crisis, many middle-class families suffered job instability and financial loss. In particular, the depreciation of the Korean won against the dollar greatly increased the financial cost of supporting families abroad. As a result, many *kirogi* parents decided to bring their children back and reenter them in Korean schools.

But that was not the entire reason for the decline of early study abroad. Another important reason was growing skepticism about the value of sending children abroad at an early age and having them graduate from American or other foreign universities. Some of the students who came back to Korea did well in the job market, cashing in on their English-language ability and foreign experience. But many did not. By the 2010s when the first batch of early study-abroad students were returning to Korea after earning bachelor's degrees, there were plenty of young people their age in the job market with a good command of English. This was largely due to the impressive growth of opportunities to learn English inside Korea—the many well-equipped private institutes, tutoring services, English kindergartens, and other venues such as "English villages," where people stay a few days and speak only English under the guidance of native speakers. Moreover, Korean universities have become internationalized at a fast rate. In response to a strong push from the government, most universities have dramatically increased courses taught in English and hired many foreign professors and instructors. At the first-tier universities, new faculty hires are now routinely tested on their ability to teach in English and are obligated to do so in a certain proportion of their courses. Many universities have also established sister relationships with foreign universities and send their students to these schools as short-term exchange students. All these institutional changes have tremendously increased the opportunities to learn and master English without leaving Korea. Thus, English fluency has slowly ceased to be a scarce commodity, reducing the advantage of overseas-educated students.

Still another more serious problem was that many of those who left Korea at an early age and lived overseas for several years had difficulty adapting to the Korean work culture, which remains far more authoritarian, overdemanding, and sexist than work cultures in most Western industrial societies. Many of the returnees from early study abroad did not stay long with the companies that hired them. The problem of adaptation seems greater in the medium-sized firms than in the large and more globalized firms because the work culture in the former tends to be more traditional and more demanding. Furthermore, those who studied abroad from an early age had not developed the social networks that are very important for an initial job search as well as later job mobility. Most of them tended to rely heavily on family networks rather than Korean school networks. A recent study on Korean returnees from study abroad found how important it is for them to possess "local cultural capital" (more than social ties) in order to successfully maneuver in the Korean job market upon their return (Jarvis 2019). In general, those students who studied abroad before graduating from a Korean university were less successful in finding satisfactory jobs than those who left after graduating from a Korean university. Jarvis (2019) thus argues that the right combination of local and global cultural capital is essential for occupational success in Korea. Waters (2009) made a similar argument in her study of Hong Kong's overseas graduates who returned home. She argues that "overseas credentials" require a certain amount of "social capital" (basically social connections) to get these credentials "valorized," that is, to be accorded value and rewarded in the local labor market.

Strategizing Global Education

We have seen that early study abroad began to lose popularity in the 2010s. This does not mean that Korean parents' eagerness to provide overseas education to their young children has diminished a lot. Such a change would be highly unlikely as long as the value of English competence and foreign degrees remains so high. What has changed in recent years is not the enthusiasm for global education but rather the approach to it, which has become better informed and far more strategic and diversified.

One important reason why early study abroad is still popular in Korea is that it provides a convenient though highly costly means for well-to-do families to avoid their children's possible failure in the educational competition in Korea. If parents have a child who is not doing well at school and is thus unlikely to make it to an elite university in Korea, their option is to send the child to the United States, Canada, Australia, or New Zealand and have her or him attend elementary or high school and advance to a university there. This is a sort of face-saving strategy for upper-middle–class parents. One parent (himself a graduate of Korea's top-ranking university) told me that he had dreaded the possibility that his son would fail to be admitted to a first-tier university in Seoul and have to attend a second-rate university in the countryside. That would have been a great embarrassment to him and his wife, he said, so he decided to send his son to the United States when he was a middle school sophomore. His son graduated from an American high school and successfully entered one of the big-ten universities in the United States. Thus, despite the high financial cost, these parents have good reason to be satisfied with the strategic decision they made for their child.

In fact, many affluent middle-class parents are using this secondary strategy as an alternative to a more ideal domestic route, which is getting admitted to one of the most prestigious private high schools, such as the Daewon Foreign Language School and the Minjok Leadership Academy, and from there making a successful passage to Seoul National University or one of the other two SKY universities. As one student I interviewed told me, the latter is the "golden path," a dream course for most middle-class parents. All the intense educational struggles are directed toward this end. But the reality is that only a tiny minority of students can travel by this golden path simply because the number of students admitted to the SKY universities is less than 3 percent of high school graduates each year. Therefore, 97 percent of high school graduates are destined to fail and must either accept admission to a lower-tier university or decide to wait and try again a year later. In fact, one important reason why Korea's *hagwons* prosper is to prepare the repeaters of college entrance exams for the next year. In the face of this reality, the globalized education market provides affluent middle-class families a convenient secondary option. For them, attending a less-known university in the United States is far more acceptable than attending a second-tier Korean university. This strategy costs the parents a lot of money, of course, but with this financial investment their children can swap a somewhat second-rate Korean degree for a more respectable degree from America or another advanced Western country. This means that early study abroad can provide a means to avoid the possibility of downward mobility for their children. A similar pattern was observed in Hong Kong by Waters (2005).

Another popular approach is to use early study abroad for a short period and bring children back home to finish their schooling in Korea. This strategy has many advantages. Children will come back home with fluent English that helps them fare much better in competing for admission to elite high schools, which put more emphasis on English ability and foreign experience more than other schools. This is a strategy used most effectively by academics, diplomats, and some corporate managers who take overseas appointments for a few years. Among Korean academics, going to the United States or other English-speaking countries on their sabbatical leaves has almost become a must not so much for their own academic purposes but for the sake of their children's education. At the end of the sabbatical leave one of the parents, most commonly the mother, may decide to stay a year or two more so the children can be immersed in English a little longer. No doubt, the children of highly educated parents who have the additional advantage of studying abroad at an early age must fare better in competition for admission to elite schools in Korea. It seems that most students in prestigious private schools such as the Daewon Foreign High School and the Minjok Leadership Academy have had at least some overseas educational experience. A graduate of one of these schools told me that she was shocked to find out that almost all of her classmates in the seventh grade had been overseas. One day her teacher asked the class how many of them had been overseas, and almost everybody except her and a couple of others raised their hand. Hearing this story, her parents (small business owners) quickly decided to give her at least one foreign trip in a hurry, so they took her on a short trip to Thailand that summer.

While there is a continuous flow of Korean students going to English-speaking countries, a recent phenomenon of significance is the rise of China as a study-abroad destination. The increasing dependence of the Korean economy on the Chinese market has made China another powerful force in Korean educational mobility. The number of Korean students going to China has increased rapidly during the past decade and a half, growing from 26,784 in 2004 to 64,400 in 2010 and declining a little to 63,937 in 2014. (The number of Korean students in China came close to the number of Korean students in the United States, which was 74,098 in 2014.) Major advantages of choosing China over the United States or other Western countries are, of course, its geographical proximity and the lower cost of studying there. In the 1990s when the flow of Korean students to China first began to swell, it was mainly due to cost considerations and the ease of admission to major universities in China. But studying in China was still considered less desirable than studying in the United States or Europe, and learning English was and still is considered more valuable than mastering Chinese. Thus, many Korean students going to China, especially those from well-off families, are attending foreign-language schools or schools that emphasize learning English in China. But in recent years as economic relations between Korea and China have deepened, many Korean parents have begun to rethink the value of learning Chinese and developing Chinese ties. Study abroad in China may be on the way to becoming more than a secondary choice, at least for business-oriented people if not for professional people.

In this regard, it is useful to observe an interesting divergence among different groups of the upper middle class in terms of their attitudes toward English-language skill and overseas education. In an interesting study conducted in the Netherlands, Weenink (2007) found a diverging pattern of educational choices between two factions of the upper middle class: the traditional elite and the new elite. While the old established elite families preferred to send their children to the traditional elite schools (gymnasiums), the new upwardly mobile elite families were more likely to send their children to international schools. Weenink suggests that the existence of these two educational choices—the established form versus the new cosmopolitan form—derives from the different assets of power possessed by the two groups of the upper middle class in the Netherlands.

For the new elite, whose power base is more globally than domestically grounded, the choice of international schools makes sense, while the established elite, whose power is based on time-honored assets and social prestige rather than global resources, continue to prefer to send their children to the gymnasiums.

A somewhat similar pattern of differences can be observed in Korea. Two neighborhoods of Gangnam reveal an interesting contrast in terms of the residents' approaches to domestic versus international education. One is Daechidong, the area where so many of the top-ranking *hagwon*s and tutorial services are concentrated, and the other is Apgujeongdong, the neighborhood famous for its fancy department stores, boutique shops, and cafés. Although residents of both areas belong to the upper middle class in Korea, they seem to make different educational choices for their children. The dominant educational goal among Daechidong parents is to send their children first to an elite private high school, then to Seoul National University or another elite university, and afterward to America for a professional degree; meanwhile, many residents of Apgujeongdong seem to choose early study abroad instead of taking a more rigorous and competitive domestic track. (The wealthiest neighborhood in Gangnam, Chungdamdong, is very similar to Apgujeongdong in this regard.) This difference is reflected in the kinds of private educational facilities dominant in the two areas. The Daechidong area is overpopulated with college-admission cram schools (aimed at the top-tier universities), while Apgujeongdong has many topnotch consulting firms that specialize in study-abroad programs. Presumably this is due to the different occupational compositions of the two areas. While Daechidong has more professional and managerial residents, Apgujeongdong has more businesspeople and independent property owners. It is understandable that business owners and wealthy property owners are less concerned about class reproduction through education because they can pass on their business ownership or income-generating property to their children. Thus, they are more relaxed about education and can encourage their children to have an interesting time abroad and bring home cosmopolitan experiences and cultural skills. In contrast, professional and managerial people know that the only way their children can inherit their parents' privileged positions is through education, so they are far more serious about their children's educational credentials.

The difference between Daechidong and Apgujeongdong, or between the professional-managerial class and the bourgeois or petite bourgeois class, however, must not be exaggerated in the context of Korea. In Korea's extremely competitive educational environment, parents would be unwise to rely on any one particular strategy of education, domestic or global, national or cosmopolitan. The merits and demerits of any particular strategy can shift quickly in changing economic contexts, as revealed in the case of early study abroad. What seemed to be a smart strategy in the early 2000s became a doubtful one by the end of the decade, though still popular among some families. Hence, Korean upper-middle-class parents remain anxious about the educational choices they make and can never be certain they are not being outsmarted by others parents. The many private consulting services that have prospered in Gangnam prey on their vulnerability. But even selecting the right consulting service is not easy and requires special information. All of these responsibilities typically fall on the mothers, generating tremendous anxieties for these so-called education moms. Gangnam moms in particular are at the forefront of the pursuit of global education, and despite their financial and informational advantages, they suffer even more uncertainty and anxiety in managing their children's education than ordinary middle-class mothers do.

Cosmopolitanism as Cultural Capital

Before Korea was fully open to the world, what counted as global skills was relatively simple, involving primarily English-language competence and foreign degrees. But with the deeper globalization of the economy and society, what is increasingly demanded and valued in the job market and social circles is a broader set of cultural knowledge and skills along with cultural tastes and lifestyles nurtured through extensive travel and educational experience abroad—something that can be called cosmopolitan cultural capital. Cosmopolitanism is thus a useful concept for considering how globalization brings new cultural qualifications for occupational success and social distinction in today's Korean society.

In the literature, "cosmopolitanism" refers to a certain moral, ethical, and philosophical orientation. In an oft-cited definition of the concept, Hannerz (1990, 239) states that "a more genuine cosmopolitanism is first of all an orientation, a willingness to engage with the Other. It is an intellectual and aesthetic stance of openness toward divergent cultural experiences, a search for contrasts rather than uniformity." Cosmopolitans are thus described as those who possess "cultivated detachment from restrictive forms of identity" (Anderson 1998) or who are at home in the cultures of other peoples as well as their own. In a more political sense, a cosmopolitan is a "person whose allegiance is to the worldwide community of human beings" (Nussbaum 1996, 4).

It is well recognized that cosmopolitanism is largely a Western cultural construct based on an elitist worldview. The ideal for this construct comes from the intellectuals and artists of the nineteenth century who gathered in such well-known cosmopolitan cities as Paris, Rome, and London, enjoying and producing high culture in the form of literature, art, and music. Recent years have seen challenges to this elitist notion of cosmopolitanism. In a sharp critique of its Western bias, James Clifford (1988, 263) argues that "the privilege of standing above cultural particularism, of aspiring to the universalist power that speaks for humanity[,] . . . is a privilege invented by a totalizing Western liberalism." Many scholars have pointed out that as far as cultural openness to foreigners and other cultures is concerned, it can be found rather easily among migrant workers and other working-class people who work and live in ethnically mixed communities. Thus, several new terms have been suggested to describe the "actually existing cosmopolitanisms" outside the Western, elitist circles such as "discrepant cosmopolitanism" (Clifford 1992), "vernacular cosmopolitanism," "banal cosmopolitanism," "working-class cosmopolitanism," and so forth (see Malcomson 1998; Robbins 1998).

What is missing in most discussions about actually existing cosmopolitanism, in my view, is the way cosmopolitanism is most typically understood in non-Western less developed societies. Cosmopolitanism in these societies often expresses the desire and aspiration to be part of advanced Western civilization. Cosmopolitanism in Korea, as in many other societies, is usually associated with extensive overseas travel and educational experiences along with the cultural knowledge and taste formed out of such experiences. It also involves competence in dealing with foreign cultures and global institutional rules. Their cultural openness, however, is directed primarily toward the Western advanced societies. So, this cosmopolitanism differs from what the early intellectuals had in mind, that is, the transcendence of local identities and genuine openness to the Other regardless of nationality, race, and religion. Lacking such a humanistic ideal or commitment, the cosmopolitanism we see in Korea is of a lifestyle rather than ethical or moral nature.

I believe there to be a similar Western-oriented cosmopolitanism in most non-Western less developed societies, which makes sense from a world-system perspective. As the world-system theorists argue, the world capitalist system is divided into three zones in terms of economic, political, and cultural power: core, periphery, and semiperiphery (Wallerstein 1974). Many highly educated citizens of periphery and semiperiphery countries who aspire to be cosmopolitan are eager to adopt the cultures and lifestyles prevalent in the metropolitan centers of the core. The ever-tighter integration of the world economy in the current era and the dominance of giant transnational corporations make it imperative for them to acquire the skills and cultural aptitudes of the core nations in order to achieve occupational success. Concretely, this involves such cultural qualifications as English fluency; college degrees from the United States, Canada, Europe, or Australia; work and life experiences in these countries; familiarity with institutional rules in advanced economies; and a network of friends across countries. This is exactly why tens of thousands of aspiring students from Asia are coming to North America and Western Europe for education and travel.

This discussion leads us to consider another important aspect of cosmopolitanism: cosmopolitanism as cultural capital. Cosmopolitanism in the actual world represents more than a philosophical or ethical stance; it involves a body of knowledge and a set of cultural skills and therefore constitutes what can be called cultural capital. Several scholars have recognized this aspect of cosmopolitanism. Hannerz (2006, 16), for example, writes that "a cosmopolitan cultural orientation in this view has gone with more formal education, more travel, more leisure as well as material resources to allow the cultivation of a knowledge of the diversity of cultural forms." Those who can obtain this cultural capacity are the ones who possess a certain amount of the material and intellectual means to do so. Calhoun (2003, 443) also points out that the acquisition of cosmopolitanism is "often made possible by capital—social and cultural as well as economic." He even argues that cosmopolitanism represents the "class consciousness of frequent travelers."

But it is in the context of the newly industrialized societies that cosmopolitanism is more often looked at as a form of cultural capital. Many scholars have characterized the growing volume of educational migration from the East Asian newly industrialized societies to North America, Europe, and Australia as a pursuit of cosmopolitan cultural capital (Park and Abelmann 2004; Matthews and Sidhu 2005; Waters 2005; Koo 2010; Kim 2011; Lan 2018; Jarvis 2019). Considering cosmopolitanism as a form of cultural capital, it is useful to recall Bourdieu's distinction of institutional cultural capital and embodied cultural capital. The former means cultural skills conferred and certified by institutions, such as academic degrees, certificates, and licenses. The latter involves language skills, cultural tastes, manner, the ability to appreciate high culture, and the like, which require a longer time to acquire and need to be embodied. We can find these two types of cosmopolitan cultural capital in any society. In Korea, we have seen that globalization has greatly increased the value of English competence and degrees from foreign schools. The globalized educational system plays a critical role in this process. As Igarashi and Saito (2014) suggest, cosmopolitanism can become powerful cultural capital when it is institutionalized through educational systems. They argue that "educational systems legitimate cosmopolitanism, a set of dispositions of openness to foreign others and cultures, as well as competences to enact such openness with ease, as universally desirable for people living in a global world" (12).

But a more subtle embodied form of cosmopolitan cultural capital is also very important, especially in the upper circles of societies. Hannerz (2006, 16) refers to this embodied cultural capital when he comments that "taking a Bourdieuan perspective, we could find cosmopolitan tastes and knowledge serving as symbolic capital in elite competitive games of distinction." Weenink (2008, 1092) also argues that cosmopolitanism represents a form of social and cultural capital, stressing especially its embodied nature (habitus) as "bodily and mental predispositions and competencies (savoir faire) which help to engage confidently in such [transnational] arenas."

In general, acquiring embodied cultural capital requires more time and resources than is the case for institutionalized cultural capital. The kind of cosmopolitan cultural capital stressed at the early stages of globalization is likely to be the institutionalized form of global skills (e.g., English fluency and foreign degrees). But at a later stage we observe that embodied cosmopolitan cultural capital (e.g., sophisticated Western-oriented cultural tastes, language patterns, lifestyle, and manner) seems to be more important as a marker of class distinction at the upper-middle–class level. A Taiwanese sociologist, Lan (2018, 53), highlights this point clearly when she describes what Taiwanese upper-middle–class parents stress when they send their children abroad for study: "The acquisition of 'Western cultural capital' not only refers to *institutionalized* forms of cultural capital, like Western degrees and credentials; it also involves *embodied* cultural capital, such as familiarity with upper-middle–class Western ways of thinking and living and the acquisition of long-lasting dispositions in the mind and body."

The same applies to Korea. When Korean parents send their children for early study abroad, they are not just interested in seeing them successful at school in America or another host country. They also expect their children to acquire many other cultural skills by getting thoroughly acquainted with the culture of the host country, gaining a broad vision of the world, and becoming comfortable in dealing with foreigners and foreign institutions. This broad set of cultural skills involves more than institutional cultural capital. A new trend that has appeared in Korea today is that embodied cosmopolitan capital is becoming increasingly important in entering professional and high-level managerial jobs and in making status claims as elite members of the society.

Conclusion

This book is about how the Korean middle class has experienced economic and social change in the era of neoliberal globalization. My main interest here is to examine how rising inequality in recent decades has led to important changes in the middle class in its internal composition, internal class dynamics, and class identity. I approach the middle class not as a fixed category but instead as a fluid and somewhat fuzzy collectivity of individuals and families occupying a broadly similar economic position in the middle of society. I also look at the middle class as a social space where competition for status, privilege, and security intensifies as economic inequality increases. Thus, the middle class provides a window through which to observe important social changes occurring in society.

Like middle classes in other advanced economies, the Korean middle class has been economically squeezed and shrinking in size. But the focus of the book is on the way the middle class has become internally differentiated between a small minority that benefits from the global economic change and a large majority that suffers from it. This internal differentiation generates a challenging dynamic within Korean society as the newly emerged affluent groups seek to distinguish themselves from the rest of the middle class and establish a new privileged class position. This book explores how these tensions play out in three areas: consumption and lifestyle, residential differentiation, and education. In all three areas, the dominant orientation of the affluent groups is to preserve their newfound privilege and pass it on to their children. The rest of the middle class tries to follow the affluent's class practices, suffering great anxiety and frustrations and observing a widening gap between themselves and the affluent minority. The affluent, while enjoying many new opportunities brought by globalization, also suffer a great deal of anxiety; this is due to the rising cost of status maintenance and the difficulties of ensuring class reproduction for their children in this age of great job insecurity.

The focus of my analysis is on the newly emerged affluent groups, as they play a dominant role in leading many changes occurring in the middle class. The emergence of the new affluent groups in Korea is the product of growing economic inequality in the era of neoliberal globalization. As we saw in chapter 2, Korea has maintained a relatively moderate level of income inequality during its rapid industrialization from the 1960s to the mid-1990s. The middle class expanded greatly during this period. But income distribution began to take a reverse course since the 1997 Asian financial crisis. Inequality has grown steadily along with the shrinking of the middle class. After Asian financial crises and the global financial crisis of 2007–2008, the Korean economy recovered and has moved successfully along a neoliberal and global model of capitalist development, becoming at the same time highly capital- and technology-intensive in its production system. This economic transformation, however, has been accompanied by rising inequality that is often described as economic polarization.

A heavy concentration of national income at the top in many advanced economies—in the upper 1 percent or, more remarkably, the 0.1 or 0.01 percent—has been well observed by many studies (see Stiglitz 2012; Piketty 2014; Milanovits 2016). The upper 1 percent in the United States is not only superrich but also wields so much influence that Stiglitz (2011) even describes America as a society "of the 1%, by the 1%, for the 1%." But it is also important to recognize that there exists in many societies another significant line of division occurring below the upper 1 percent. Reeves (2017a, 6) made this point most clearly: "It is not just the 'upper class' that has been flourishing. A much broader swath of American society is doing well—and detaching themselves." His analysis demonstrates that the share of income received by the upper 10–20 percent of income earners has increased in recent decades, while income going to the middle-income groups has declined significantly.

Korea's income distribution over the past two decades reveals the same pattern as that of the United States. Like in America and many other advanced economies, the dominant pattern of income inequality in Korea in recent decades was the extraordinary income concentration at the top, the upper 1 percent or 0.1 percent. But at the same time, Korean data also suggest that the upper 10–20 percent of income earners have seen their incomes rising fast during the past two decades, while the rest have experienced a declining or stagnating income situation. Therefore, we can look at the economic polarization in Korea as involving two tiers: at the first tier we have the division between the top 1 percent and the bottom 99 percent, while at the second tier we have the division between the upper 10–20 percent and the bottom 80–90 percent. This book is mainly interested in the social implications of the second form of polarization. The first form of polarization is, of course, very important because the superrich wield so much power to influence the economic and political systems. But I choose to focus on the second form of polarization because this inequality is directly relevant to understanding the changing class relations in the middle of society.

In most conventional economic analyses, the upper 10–20 percent of income earners is most often looked at as the upper-income group. And economists like to interpret their income growth in contrast to income reduction among the next four decile groups as an empirical confirmation of the middle-class squeeze thesis. But I have argued in this book that it would be more appropriate to regard this upper 10–20 percent as part of the middle class, more specifically as the upper-middle or affluent middle class. From this perspective, the rise of the upper 10–20 percent of income earners in the midst of the declining incomes of the lower income groups can be better understood as the internal division occurring within the middle class rather than the decline of the middle class as a whole. I regard the upper 10 percent of income earners as constituting the upper middle class. Using the upper 10 percent or 20 percent or even the upper 5 percent to identify the upper middle class is somewhat arbitrary. However, as I suggested in chapter 2, if we take both income and wealth, not just income, as a measure of class position, it is more reasonable to take the upper 10 percent as representing the upper middle class.

My major interest in this book, however, is not to propose any fine classification scheme of Korea's class structure or to look for the causal factors of economic polarization but rather to explore the social implications of economic polarization for the middle class as well as the whole society. To investigate the changing class dynamics occurring in the middle class as a consequence of rising inequality, I have directed attention to three dimensions of social life: consumption, residential differentiation, and educational practices. Analytically speaking, what is happening in consumption and residential differentiation represents a class-distinction process represented by a desire among those in the affluent middle class to separate themselves from the ordinary middle class. And what is happening in the educational field can be understood as class-reproduction struggles involving well-to-do parents' efforts to pass their status onto children through education. In these three areas, we can observe how widening inequality in the middle has brought a new pattern of status competition and a new type of struggles to secure advantaged positions or not to be left behind. The nature of the middle class and its social meaning for society has also changed because of this process.

Consumption is a major area in which class distinction occurs most vividly. Korea's newly emerged affluent groups sought to use conspicuous consumption first to distinguish themselves from the ordinary middle class. This began to appear most visibly after the state lifted a ban on imports of consumer goods in the early 1980s and allowed the influx of luxury goods from abroad. The marketing industry quickly introduced the label *myongpoom* (implying high-quality goods) to distinguish luxury goods from those domestically produced. The *myongpoom* label was attached to all kinds of luxury imports carrying the prestigious logos of Louis Vuitton, Gucci, Chanel, Prada, Hermes, and the like. Korean consumers' craze with *myongpoom* goods lasted about a decade or two but began to subside slowly. By that time, most conventional *myongpoom* goods became too widely available to middle-class people, though mostly in the form of counterfeits, and ceased to serve as a status marker for the affluent middle class. This made the well-to-do seek a more expensive and prestigious grade of *myongpoom* goods or try to find products that are more scarce and exclusive and are beyond the reach of ordinary consumers.

Along with this rising standard of luxury goods, another area of class distinction occurred in less conspicuous but more substantial areas of middle-class lifestyle. From the 1990s, well-being became a major obsession among affluent middle-class families. They became keenly interested in eating organic foods and many imported health foods. The middle-class shopping pattern has also changed. The well-to-do prefer to shop at stores that carry only premier-quality products or order custom-made products from the producers directly, while others shop at neighborhood supermarkets. The quality of foods targeted at the affluent continued to improve, while Korea's superefficient home delivery system made it easy for them to enjoy good foods without leaving home. The COVID-19 pandemic made class difference in this area more apparent and consequential. The well-to-do can have high-quality groceries and prepared foods delivered quickly to their homes through telephone or Internet ordering, while most other middle-class people continue to rely on traditional shopping at crowded supermarkets. As in the United States, Korea's consumer market became slowly divided between the upscale and downscale markets, putting more focus on production of goods and services for the affluent at the expense of the rest of the middle as well as the lower class. Those in the latter groups are therefore forced to follow the consumption pattern of the affluent, suffering more strain on their family budgets.

Another interesting trend that appeared in recent years is Korean people's obsession with physical appearance and their willingness to spend lots of money and time to achieve a good look and youthful-looking skin. Increasingly, the idea of luxury and high status is extended to health and body maintenance. If luxury meant the possession of luxury goods yesterday, now it meant how to use them and also how to carry them on our bodies. In order to claim a high status, one now needs to possess a well-maintained, relatively slim, and sophisticated-looking body. This new trend has been actively promoted by Korea's famed cosmetic surgery and skin care services. Both the well-to-do and the less well-off became captives of this new trend and spend more money than they need to. But obviously, they receive class-divided services depending on their income levels.

In relation to consumption, residential separation has become an important phenomenon in Korea in recent years. The emergence of Gangnam is particularly important in this regard. Gangnam is the product of the state's aggressive urban project to construct the most modern and global city that can showcase Korea's economic miracle to the world. The state made enormous infrastructural investment in this area and provided various policy supports to facilitate the construction of this area in a short period of time. The state also used its muscle to relocate elite high schools and major cultural facilities from Gangbuk to Gangnam in order to induce middle-class residents to move to Gangnam.

Once Gangnam began to take shape as a new city (within the Seoul metropolitan area), real estate prices there began to rise fast. And over the past four decades, Gangnam's real estate prices have never failed to grow faster than in other areas in the country. Consequently, those who moved to Gangnam early enough benefited tremendously from the continuously rising real estate values of the area. Even many of those who moved there later could ride on the rising curve of the housing market in the area. The most important trigger of this continuous rise in Gangnam's real estate values is the congregation of good schools and top-notch private educational facilities (*hagwons*). Given the importance of private supplementary education for getting into elite universities in Korea, middle-class families are all eager to move to this area despite its overpriced housing market.

In the earlier years of its development, Gangnam distinguished itself mainly as a fashionable consumption place. All the new trends of fashion and luxury consumption started from here, and the busy streets of Gangnam are covered with fancy restaurants, cafés, bars, boutique shops, hair salons, beauty clinics, and entertainment places. But entering the twenty-first century, Gangnam gradually turned into a high-tech and global business center, drawing many international financial firms (banks, insurance firms, investment and accounting services) and flagship stores of global brand-name products. Thus, in many ways Gangnam has become a full-fledged global city, offering better job market opportunities to young people especially in terms of access to more desirable professional and technical jobs in the globalized sector.

By the early 2000s Gangnam had thus established itself as a sort of model city of the nation, possessing many good things that are desired by urban residents: superior infrastructure, good schools and top-rated cram schools, the most modern living environment, and most of all the continuous appreciation of real estate values. Thus, residing in Gangnam, especially in its wealthier neighborhoods, is considered a privilege despite the materialistic and vulgar aspects of Gangnam culture. Thus, non-Gangnam residents look at Gangnam people with envy and jealousy, admiration and resentment. Whether they like it or not, most middle-class Koreans desire to move to Gangnam at least for the sake of their children's education. But given the current housing market in the area, it is now almost impossible for average middle-income earners to move to Gangnam. In many ways, this mobility barrier between Gangnam and non-Gangnam areas symbolizes the sharpening class boundary between the affluent and privileged segment of the middle class and the rest of the middle in Korea today.

After examining class distinction process occurring through consumption and residential separation, I devoted close attention to the changing class practices in the area of education. Children's education has long been a main concern among middle-class parents. While Korean parents of all classes are well known for their high educational aspiration for children, it is the middle class that is more preoccupied with education than other classes. And within the middle class, it is the upper-middle–class parents who are most anxious to see their children succeed in educational competition so they can inherit the parents' status. Thus, the rise of the affluent middle class and the widening economic gap between this group and the rest of the middle class had important consequences for the evolving educational competition in Korea. This occurred mainly through the development of private supplementary education outside the school system. Wealthy families always sought private tutorial education in order to increase the competitive edge of their children. But it was the state's ambitious effort, well intended but misguided, to remove differences between elite and other high schools and create an equalized high school system, the HSEP. The policy backfired, however, as affluent parents lost trust in the public schools and tried to buy more competitive education in the private market. The result was the rise of the huge uncontrollable private-education industry. The role these private educational facilities play increased as the universities tried to develop a more rational and democratic system of student screening, often following the American model. The most significant consequence of this development was that children's educational success came to depend on parents' financial status more than on their own efforts and talents.

In the post-1990 era, it was the globalization of the Korean economy that came to influence Korea's educational change more than domestic factors. The most notable change after Korea's march to globalization was the rise of English and global skills as critical educational credentials for occupational success. This trend triggered a wave of educational migration of young children, often accompanied by their mothers, to English-speaking countries. Obviously it was the well-to-do families who led this global educational strategy, but less well-off middle-class families followed the strategy even though doing so meant playing a losing game. Both the form and content of global education have constantly evolved as the educational struggle shifted ground, producing uncertain consequences for both students and parents. What is certain, however, is that globalized education today works to accentuate class differences in educational opportunities between affluent professional and managerial families and the rest of the middle class.

Increasing class competition in the global environment, however, does not always bring benefits and success to affluent people. Though more advantaged, they are not exempt from the increasing anxiety and uncertainty that economic change brings in this global era. The economic instability and relative deprivation experienced by the lower-middle class are easy to understand. But interestingly enough, there is no less anxiety and frustration among the affluent middle class. Their sources of anxiety are different in that they need to keep ahead in the escalating status competition and constantly look for better educational opportunities for their children in the increasingly privatized and globalized education market. Although they make tremendous investments in time, money, and gathering information for their children's education, there is no guarantee that these investments will pay off, as the job market in Korea has become tighter and more competitive. In a sense, all members of the Korean middle class are caught in what Brown (2003, 142) calls the "opportunity trap," whereby "middle-class families are adopting more desperate measures to win a positional advantage. They are having to run faster, for longer, just to stand still. . . . If all adopt the same tactics nobody gets ahead." What Brown describes in the context of Great Britain occurs exactly the same in Korea today. Although the affluent and globalized middle class can be considered the winners of the globalized game of competition, the costs of class reproduction through global strategies are simply too high and the returns too uncertain. Thus, both the winners and the losers of neoliberal globalization suffer from great anxiety and frustration.

The internal division of the middle class and increased competition among its members had important consequences for class identity in the Korean middle class. In the old days, the social meaning of the middle class was largely unproblematic. It was understood broadly as a class of individuals and families enjoying a certain degree of economic comfort and leeway and being able to participate in mainstream social and cultural activities, and there was a shared understanding of what kind of socioeconomic standards must be met to belong to this category. But with the growing divergence within the middle class, especially the rise of the affluent and privileged group and its gradual separation from the larger middle class, it became unclear who really represents the middle class today. Gradually, the lifestyle and social mobility strategies of the affluent families have come to define the standards of respectable middle-class membership. Meanwhile, the majority of the middle class, who are becoming squeezed by precarious jobs, rising prices, and increasing family debt, have become deeply frustrated and anxious and must wonder whether they are still middle class. But those who are lucky enough to see their income and financial assets growing realize they have less and less in common with most other middle-class people and desire to separate themselves from these ordinary middle-class people. Consequently, the middle class is gradually losing both its top and bottom tiers; the affluent and privileged group is pulled upward, probably preferring to identify themselves with the upper class or the global middle class, while those at the lower end are pulled down. Even members of the stable middle (or the middle middle) are becoming unsure of their position, because of their slipping economic condition and their sense of relative deprivation vis-à-vis the affluent minority above them. In the eyes of most people, including those who would otherwise make the core members of the middle class, today it is affluent people who seem to represent the true middle class in Korea. In short, recent economic change in the neoliberal era has rendered the Korean middle class increasingly polarized, muddled, and somewhat vacuous. Clearly, it is no longer the relatively homogeneous, fluid, and upwardly mobile class that it was in the past.

From a broad theoretical point of view, my book is concerned with the question of class distinction, about which Pierre Bourdieu developed an elaborate theory. Bourdieu's theoretical ideas informed my analysis in many ways. His conceptualization of class as resulting from the distribution of three forms of capital—economic, cultural, and social—and the convertibility of different forms of capital from economic to social and cultural, or vice versa, helped in my analysis of Korea's changing class relations. And like Bourdieu, I approached the middle class as a social space rather than a fixed category with clear boundaries. The objective of my analysis was to examine what was occurring in the middle space of society as a consequence of rising inequality in the global era. I suggested that many of the new class practices employed by the affluent segment of the middle class could be understood as efforts to convert their economic capital into social and cultural capital.

Bourdieu's theory of class distinction, however, is primarily focused on cultural and symbolic processes, despite his insistence that economic capital is always at the root of symbolic power. The most crucial element of his explanation of class distinction is his unique concept of habitus, a class-specific system of durable dispositions or a scheme of perceptions, thought, and behavior. Habitus is rooted in one's material condition but is shaped through socialization at home and in schools. Once it becomes internalized or embodied, habitus has a powerful effect on the individual's perceptions, actions, and social relations. In his masterful work *Distinction*, Bourdieu thus gives primary attention to how habitus works to differentiate classes and functions as a mechanism of class reproduction.

Bourdieu's analysis of French society with these cultural concepts is certainly interesting and convincing, but I have some reservation about applying his overly culturalist approach directly to newly industrialized societies such as Korea. I believe that Bourdieu put too much emphasis on cultural mechanisms of class production, paying far less attention to the role of structural and institutional factors. As we know, the popularity of his theories coincided with the cultural turn in sociology in recent years.

As Bourdieu acknowledged, class habitus is not simply determined by the material condition of existence. In societies such as France, what Bourdieu calls the "legitimate" culture of the dominant class provided a major frame of reference for other classes. But most societies that have undergone dramatic industrial transformation in recent decades have not maintained a hegemonic cultural system, and the class habitus of the upper middle class, if it exists, is likely to be no more than a recently adopted and relatively shallow experience of lifestyles, tastes, and cultural knowledge borrowed from the West. In fact, many of the new rich's cultural tastes—expressed, for example, in providing piano and violin lessons for their children, attending expensive concerts, taking overseas leisure trips, practicing yoga, and playing golf—are very likely to be advantages that can be purchased easily with money. Therefore, I do not regard class habitus as the most useful conceptual tool for understanding the class distinction process in Korean society.

Instead, my book pays closer attention to the changing class relations at the economic and social levels, focusing on the efforts of the newly emerged affluent groups to seek more privileged opportunities in the consumption and educational markets. The struggles for more advantaged educational opportunities for children represent the focal point of class struggles in Korea today. And this struggle occurs through private supplementary education more than through parental upbringing of children. This suggests that money plays a more important role than class culture in Korea. Money can buy privileged educational opportunities that help one's children acquire a better education and higher cultural capital, which then facilitate class reproduction. This market mechanism must operate in any capitalist society. But in mature capitalism, the privileged class has developed some institutional and cultural means to maintain their privileges (such as exclusionary zoning and college legacy preferences in the United States). In contrast, class distinction has occurred in Korea without such institutional or cultural mechanisms to support the widening inequality. Consequently, the changing class relations in Korea have generated a great sense of relative deprivation and resentment among the losers of global economic change and also much anxiety and uncertainty among the winners of this economic process.

Notes

1. THE RISE AND FALL OF THE KOREAN MIDDLE CLASS

1. This economic way of conceptualizing the middle class is common in all East Asian societies. In Japan, the middle class is most frequently called *chusan kaikyu* or *churyu kaikyu* (Ishida and Slater 2010), with a similar meaning to that of Korea's *chungsancheung*. China also conceptualized the middle class in a predominantly economic term, calling it *zhongchan jiceng* (middle-income stratum) or *xin zhongchan jieceng* (new middle class) (Li 2010).

2. Gordon (2002, 124) observes that in Japan, "patterns of social thought and behavior that have come to define the Japanese middle class (both in Japan and abroad) came together in the high-growth era of the late 1950s through the 1970s." Kelly (2002, 235) argues that "Japan as a '90% middle-class society' has been the consistent claim for three decades, although the real effect of this 'mainstream' identification has been to 'declass' and 'massify' the debates about social stratification."

3. The level of middle-class identification varied greatly depending on how the sample was selected and how survey questions were phrased. To give some examples, 75 percent of the sample identified themselves as *chungsancheung* in a Gallup survey (in 1989), 86.8 percent did so in a study by Hong (in 1992), 70.7 percent did so in a *JoongAng Daily* survey (in 1994), 75.0 percent did so in a *Chosun Daily* survey (in 1995), 75.3 percent did so in a Hyundai Research Institute survey (in 1995), 92.4 percent did so in a *Dong-A Daily* survey (in 1995), and 77.0 percent did so in a *Hankyurae Daily* survey (in 1998).

4. What Owensby (1999, 8) describes about the Mexican middle class applies to most other societies in the Third World: "Through newspapers, books, magazines, advertisements, radio shows, photographs, and movies, Brazilians came into contact with the idea of what it was to be modern. It was an idea that took life from the visions of modernity issuing from New York, Paris, and London."

5. In 1996 the number of "good jobs" was 5.35 million, but the number of college graduates in the labor force was 4.97 million. But by 2010 the "good jobs" had increased only slightly to 5.81 million, while the number of college graduates spiked to 9.65 million, creating an oversupply of about 4 million highly skilled workers (Um 2015).

6. The same argument is made by Cho and Choi (2016, 57): "the children's generation which failed to make a (satisfactory) entrance to society must depend on the parent generation economically, and therefore, their economic troubles lead to the parents' economic burdens. When it becomes realistically difficult to achieve middle-class reproduction across generations, a sense of middle-class crisis deepens even if the parents are currently remaining in the middle class."

7. The profile of the average middle-class family in the 2010s was a three-person family with dual-income, university-educated parents in their late forties. In contrast, the 1990 profile was a four-person family with a single income from a high school–educated head of household in his late thirties (HRI 2015).

8. When asked to identify their status in terms of broad social categories of upper, middle, and lower, 77 percent of those in the objectively defined working class placed themselves in the "middle level" (different from "the middle class") in the 1990s.

2. RISING INEQUALITY

1. This chapter is a modified version of my earlier publication, Koo (2021).
2. Korea's income share among the rich was similar to that of the Japanese pattern in the 1980s, but the Korean pattern began to diverge from that of Japan and followed the same steep upward curve as found in the United States. In terms of the ratio of the top 10 percent divided by the bottom 10 percent income share, Korea's inequality (4.78) came very close to that of the United States (4.89) around 2010 (Kim and Kim 2015).
3. According to Kim and Kim (2015, 16), "Without mature manager markets in Korea, large corporations, particularly Chaebols having many affiliated companies, activated the internal labor markets for corporate officers, delegated management to professional officers, and controlled them through monitoring and performance-based rewards. Many CEOs in large corporations received exceptional pay raises along with stock options."
4. The Korean government takes 50–150 percent of the median income as the official measure of the middle class (*chungsancheung*).
5. The most recent study of the middle class by the OECD research team (OECD 2019), cited at the outset of this book, adjusted the middle-income category more highly as those in the 75–200 percent income bracket. The study subdivided the middle-income category into three groups: lower-middle income (75% to 100% of median), middle-middle income (100% to 150% of median), and upper-middle income (150% to 200% of median).

4. CLASS MAKING, GANGNAM STYLE

1. One major housing project, for example, was named like a military operation as "The 180-Day Operation of Housing Construction."
2. The primary agent in this dealing was the mayor of metropolitan Seoul, who purchased a large piece of land in Gangnam in the early 1960s and sold it in the early stages of Gangnam's development, donating the entire profits to Park Chung Hee's political fund (Son 2003; Ji 2017).
3. Since the 1980s the prices of Gangnam apartments have never fallen, even during economic downturns, and the apartments are always easier to sell than other properties. Due to its high liquidity value, Gangnam apartment ownership has been equated to ownership of blue-chip stock such as that of Samsung and other companies with reliable and high-yielding profits.
4. As Bae and Joo (2019, 14–15) report, "roughly one third of national inheritance taxpayers (31.3% based on 2016 data) and national comprehensive real estate holding taxpayers (35.8% based on 2007 data) are from the three districts. They also house 18% of Korea's *super rich*—those who hold more than 1 million USD in cash. Consider these percentages against the fact that the combined population of the three districts is a mere 3% of the total national population."
5. Kim's report (2013) in *Seoul Daily* indicated that in 2011, the chance of getting admitted to Seoul National University was seven times higher for Gangnam high school graduates than for non-Gangnam high school graduates.

5. EDUCATIONAL CLASS STRUGGLE

1. In fact, some research demonstrates that Korean parents have even higher educational aspirations for their children than Japanese parents (Nakamura 2005).
2. The most well-known international test is PISA (Program for International Student Assessment) run by the OECD, which tests 15-year students in reading, math, and

science. As Kim (2010) reports, "In PISA 2006, Korea ranked first in reading, second in math, and between 7th and 13th in science among 57 participating countries."

3. Complaints about education are stronger among middle-class people than other groups. See Hong (2005).

4. Ewha Womans University was among the elite schools until recently but has lost status with the growing preference for coeducational schools, while the private Sungkyunkwan University, which has strong financial sponsorship from the Samsung conglomerate, is rapidly catching up with other elite universities in terms of its research record and scholarly reputation.

5. Another Korean school whose name is not mentioned in the *Wall Street Journal* article is the Minjok Leadership Academy.

6. Korea's private education expenditure exceeded that of the United States, Australia, Canada, and Japan and was four times higher than the OECD average in 2006 (Kim 2010).

References

Abelmann, Nancy, Nichole Newendorp, and Sangsook Lee-Chung. 2014. "East Asia's Astronaut and Geese Families: Hong Kong and South Korean Cosmopolitanisms." *Critical Asian Studies* 46(2): 259–86.

Abelmann, Nancy, So Jin Park, and Hyunhee Kim. 2009. "College Rank and Neoliberal Subjectivity in South Korea: The Burden of Self-development." *Inter-Asia Cultural Studies* 10(2): 229–47.

Anderson, Amanda. 1998. "Cosmopolitanism, Universalism, and the Divided Legacies of Modernity." In *Cosmopolitics: Thinking and Feeling beyond the Nation*, ed. Pheng Cheah and Bruce Robbins, 265–89. Minneapolis: University of Minnesota Press.

Bae, Yooil, and Yumin Joo. 2019. "The Making of Gangnam: Social Construction and Identity of Urban Space in South Korea." *Urban Affairs Review* 56(3): 726–57.

Birdsall, Nancy, Carol Graham, and Stefano Pettinato. 2000. "Stuck in the Tunnel: Is Globalization Muddling the Middle Class?" Center on Social and Economic Dynamics, Brookings Institution, Working paper No. 14. https://pdfs.semanticscholar.org/10a1/12b075e28806c7d8a99731038782385d68d2.pdf.

Blumin, Stuart. 1989. *The Emergence of the Middle Class: Social Experience in the American City, 1760–1900*. New York: Cambridge University Press.

Bourdieu, Pierre. 1984. *Distinction: A Social Critique of the Judgement of Taste*. Cambridge, MA: Harvard University Press.

——. 1987. "What Makes a Social Class? On the Theoretical and Practical Existence of Groups." *Berkeley Journal of Sociology* 32: 1–18.

Brown, Phillip. 2003. "The Opportunity Trap: Education and Employment in a Global Economy." *European Educational Research Journal* 2(1): 141–79.

Calhoun, Craig. 2003. "The Class Consciousness of Frequent Travellers: Towards a Critique of Actually Existing Cosmopolitanism." In *Debating Cosmopolitics*, ed. Daniele Archibugi, 86–116. London: Verso.

Chadha, Radha, and Paul Husband. 2006. *The Cult of the Luxury Brand: Inside Asia's Love Affair with Luxury*. London: Nicholas Brealey International.

Chang, Ha Sung. 2015. *Wae bunno haeya haneunga* [Why Must Get Angry]. Seoul: Heisbooks.

Chang, Kyung-Sup. 1997. "Modernity through the Family: Familial Foundations of Korean Society." *International Review of Sociology* 7: 51–63.

——. 2010. *South Korea under Compressed Modernity: Familial Political Economy in Transition*. London: Routledge.

——. 2018. *Naeil ui Jongeon? Kajok chayu juuiwa sahoe chaesaengsan yiki* [The End of Tomorrow? Familial Liberalism and Social Reproduction]. Seoul: Jinmoondang.

Chang, Se-Hoon. 2017. "Chungsancheung projectroseo 'bundang mandeulki'" [Bundang Making as a Middle-class Project]. In *Gangnam mandeulki wa Gangnam ddarahaki* [Making Gangnam, Following Gangnam], ed. Bae Kyun Park and Jin Tae Hwang, 355–93. Seoul: Dongnyuk.

Chee, Maria W. L. 2003. "Migrating for the Children: Taiwanese American Women in Transnational Families." In *Wife or Worker?: Asian Women and Migration*, ed. N. Piper and M. Roces, 137–56. Lanham, MD: Rowman & Littlefield.

Cheon, Byung You, ed. 2016. *Han'guk ui bulpyeongdeung, 2016* [Inequality in Korea, 2016]. Seoul: Paper Road.
Cheon, Byung You, and Jin Wook Shin, eds. 2016. *Dajung kyeokcha: Han'guk sahoe bulpyeongdeung kujo* [Multiple Differentials: The Structure of Inequality in Korean Society]. Seoul: Paper Road.
Cho, Hae-joang. 2015. "Spec Generation Who Cannot Say 'No': Overeducated and Underemployed Youth in Contemporary South Korea." *Positions* 23(3): 437–62.
Cho, Kwon-Jung, and Ji-Won Choi. 2016. *Chungsancheung: Heundeulineun sinwha* [The Middle Class: A Flickering Myth]. Seoul: Seoul Institute.
Cho, Myung Rae. 2004. "Sin sangryucheung ui bangjuroseo ui Gangnam" [Gangnam as a Biblical Boat of the New Upper Middle Class]. *Hwanghae Munhwha* [Hwanghae Culture] 42(3): 25–40.
Cho, Uhn. 2005. "The Encroachment of Globalization into Intimate Life: The Flexible Korean Family in 'Economic Crisis.'" *Korea Journal* 45(3): 8–35.
Chosun Ilbo. 2005. "A Country Obsessed with Looks." *Chosun Ilbo* (English Edition), August 8. http://english.chosun.com/site/data/html_dir/2005/08/08/2005080861015.html.
Chua, Beng-Huat, ed. 2000. *Consumption in Asia: Lifestyles and Identities*. New York: Routledge.
Chung, Ku-Hyun, W. Kang, E. Kim, C. Han, W. Tae, J. Kim, S. Bae, H. Kang, and M. Lee. 2008. *Han'guk ui Kieop 20 nyeon* [Corporate Management in Korea, Past 20 Years]. Seoul: SERI.
Clifford, James. 1988. *The Predicament of Culture: Twentieth-Century Ethnography, Literature, and Art*. Cambridge, MA: Harvard University Press.
———. 1992. "Traveling Cultures." In *Cultural Studies*, ed. Lawrence Grossberg, Cary Nelson, and Paula Treichler, 96–112. New York: Routledge.
Currid-Halkett, Elizabeth. 2017. *The Sum of Small Things: A Theory of the Aspirational Class*. Princeton, NJ: Princeton University Press.
Davidoff, Leonore, and Catherine Hall. 1987. *Family Fortunes: Men and Women of the English Middle Class, 1780–1850*. London: Hutchinson Education.
Derne, Steve. 2005. "Globalization and the Making of a Transnational Middle Class: Implications for Class Analysis." In *Critical Globalization Studies*, ed. Richard Appelbaum and William Robinson, 177–86. New York: Routledge.
Douglass, Mike. 2006. "Global Householding in Pacific Asia." *International Review of Development and Planning* 28 (Winter): 421–45.
Ehrenreich, Barbara. 1989. *Fear of Falling: The Inner Life of the Middle Class*. New York: Harper Perennial.
Fernandes, Leela. 2006. *India's New Middle Class: Democratic Politics in an Era of Economic Reform*. Minneapolis: University of Minnesota Press.
Finch, John, and Seung-kyung Kim. 2012. "Kirŏgi Families in the US: Transnational Migration and Education." *Journal of Ethnic and Migration Studies* 38(3): 485–506.
Frank, Robert. 2007. *Falling Behind: How Rising Inequality Harms the Middle Class*. Berkeley: University of California Press.
Frykman, Jonas, and Orvar Löfgren. 1987. *Culture Builders: A Historical Anthropology of Middle-Class Life*. Translated by Alan Crozier. New Brunswick, NJ: Rutgers University Press.
Garrett, Geoffrey. 2004. "Globalization's Missing Middle." *Foreign Affairs* 83(6): 84–96.
Gelézeau, Valérie. 2007. *Apateu konghwaguk* [The Republic of Apartments]. Seoul. Humanitas. Original version published in France as *Séoul, ville géante, cités radieuses* (Paris: CNRS Éditions, 2003).
Goodman, David. 2014. *Class in Contemporary China*. Cambridge, UK: Polity.

Gordon, Andrew. 2002. "The Short Happy Life of the Japanese Middle Class." In *Social Contracts under Stress*, ed. Olivier Zunz, Leonard Schoppa, and Nobuhiro Hiwatari, 108–29. New York: Russell Sage Foundation.

Guibernau, Montserrat. 2008. "National Identity versus Cosmopolitan Identity." In *Cultural Politics in a Global Age: Uncertainty, Solidarity, and Innovation*, ed. David Held and Henrietta Moore, 148–56. Oxford, UK: Oneworld Publications.

Ham, In-Hee, Dong-Won Lee, and Sungwoong Park. 2001. *Chungsancheung ui cheongcheseong kwa sobi munhwa* [Middle Class Identity and Consumption Culture]. Seoul: Jipmundang.

Han, Wan-Sang, Tae-Hwan Kwon, and Doo-Seung Hong. 1987. "Han'guk ui chungsancheung" [The Korean Middle Class]. In *Korean Middle Classes: Research Data Book II on Korean Society in Transition*. Seoul: Hankook Ilbo.

Hannerz, Ulf. 1990. "Cosmopolitans and Locals in World Culture." *Theory, Culture & Society* 7: 237–51.

———. 2006. "Two Faces of Cosmopolitanism: Culture and Politics." CIDOB, June. https://www.cidob.org/en/publications/past_series/documents/intercultural_dynamics/two_faces_of_cosmopolitanism_culture_and_politics.

Hart, Dennis. 2001. *From Tradition to Consumption: Construction of a Capitalist Culture in South Korea*. Somerset, NJ: Jimoondang International.

Harvey, David. 2005. *A Short History of Neoliberalism*. Oxford: Oxford University Press.

Heiman, Rachel, Carla Freeman, and Mark Liechty, eds. 2012. *The Global Middle Classes: Theorizing through Ethnography*. Santa Fe, NM: School for Advanced Research Press.

Hong, Doo-Seung. 2005. *Han'guk ui chungsancheung* [The Korean Middle Class]. Seoul: Seoul National University Press.

Hong, Euny. 2014. *The Birth of Korean Cool: How One Nation Is Conquering the World through Pop Culture*. New York: Pacador.

Hong, Min Ki. 2015. "Choesangyui sodeuk bijung ui changki chuse, 1958–2013" [The Long-Term Trend of Top Income Share, 1958–2013]. *Saneop Nodong Yeongu* [Industrial Labor Study] 21(1): 191–220.

HRI. 1999. *Ilban kakye chungsancheung ui Uisik chosa'e kwanhan chosa bokiseo* [Survey Report on Middle-Class Identity among Ordinary Households]. Seoul: Hyundai Research Institute.

———. 2013. "OECD kijun chungsancheung kwa chegam chungsancheung ui koeri" [Discrepancy between Chungsancheung by the OECD definition and Subjective Chungsancheung]. *Hyeonan kwa Kwaje* [Current Issues and Tasks]. 13–02. August. Seoul: Hyundai Research Institute.

———. 2015. "Urinara chungsancheung sarm ui jil pyeonhwa" [The Changing Quality of Life among the Korean Middle Class]. *Hyeonan kwa Kwaje* [Current Issues and Tasks]. 15–06. February. Seoul: Hyundai Research Institute.

Hsiao, Hsin-Huang Michael, ed. 1999. *East Asian Middle Classes in Comparative Perspective*. Taipei: Academia Sinica.

———, ed. 2001. *Exploration of the Middle Classes in Southeast Asia*. Taipei: Academia Sinica.

Igarashi, Hiroki, and Hiro Saito. 2014. "Cosmopolitanism as Cultural Capital: Exploring the Intersection of Globalization, Education and Stratification." *Cultural Sociology* 8(3): 222–39.

Ishida, Hiroshi, and David Slater, eds. 2010. *Social Class in Contemporary Japan: Structures, Sorting and Strategies*. New York: Routledge.

Jarvis, Jonathan. 2019. "Lost in Translation: Obstacles to Converting Global Cultural Capital to Local Occupational Success." *Sociological Perspectives* 63(2): 228–48.

REFERENCES

Ji, Joo Hyung. 2017. "Gangnam kaebal kwa Gangnamjeok dosiseong ui hyeongseong" [Gangnam Development and the Formation of Gangnam-style Urbanism]. In *Gangnam mandeulki wa Gangnam ddarahaki* [Making Gangnam, Following Gangnam], ed. Bae Kyun Park and Jin Tae Hwang, 179–230. Seoul: Dongnyuk.

JoonAng Daily. 2006. "2006 sinyeon kihoek chungsancheung doesalija" [2006 New Year Special Let's Restore Chungsancheung]. January 2. https://blog.naver.com/chilship/140021104336.

Joo, Sang Young. 2015. "Piketty ironeuro bon han'guk ui punbae munje" [Distribution Problem in Korea as Seen from Piketty's Theory]. *Kyeongje Baljeon Yeonku* [Economic Development Research] 21: 21–76.

Jung, EeHwan. 2013. *Han'guk ui koyong chejeron* [The Korean Employment System]. Seoul: Humanitas.

Kang, Jun Man. 2006. *Gangnam, natseon Taehanminguk ui chahwasang* [Gangnam: An Unfamiliar Self-Portrait of Korea]. Seoul: Inmul kwa Sasangsa.

Kang, Nae Hee. 2004. "Gangnam ui kyekeup kwa munhwa" [Social Class and Culture in Gangnam]. *Hwanghae Munhwa* [Hwanghae Culture] 42(3): 62–84.

Kelly, William. 2002. "At the Limits of New Middle-Class Japan: Beyond 'Mainstream Consciousness.'" In *Social Contracts under Stress*, ed. Olivier Zunz, Leonard Schoppa, and Nobuhiro Hiwatari, 232–54. New York: Russell Sage Foundation.

Kendall, Laurel. 1996. *Getting Married in Korea: Of Gender, Morality, and Modernity*. Berkeley: University of California Press.

Kharas, Homi. 2017. "The Unprecedented Expansion of the Global Middle Class: An Update." Global Economy & Development Working Paper 100. Washington DC: Brookings Institution.

Kharas, Homi, and Geoffrey Gertz. 2010. "The New Global Middle Class: A Crossover from West to East." In *China's Emerging Middle Class: Beyond Economic Transformation*, ed. Cheng Li, 32–54. Washington, DC: Brookings Institution.

Kim, Andrew Eungi. 2004. "The Social Perils of the Korean Financial Crisis." *Journal of Contemporary Asia* 34(2): 221–37.

Kim, Byung-soo, and Ji-hoon Park. 2019. "Chungsancheung'i molakhanda" [The Middle Class Is Collapsing]. *Maeil Kyungje*, October 28. https://www.mk.co.kr/news/print/2019/881582.

Kim, Dong-hyun. 2013. "Owe Gangnamgu ui Seoul Daehak yipaklyul eun 7 bae nopeulgga" [Why Gangnam-gu's Seoul National University Enrollment Rate Is 7 Times Higher]. *Seoul Daily*, January 17. https://www.seoul.co.kr/news/newsView.php?id=20130117003003.

Kim, Eun Sil. 2004. *Sakyoyuk 1 beonji daechidong eommadeul ui ipsi cheonryak* [College Admission Strategy of Daechidong Mothers in the Educational District Number 1]. Seoul: Izibook.

Kim, Jongyoung. 2011. "Aspiration for Global Cultural Capital in the Stratified Realm of Global Higher Education: Why Do Korean Students Go to US Graduate Schools?" *British Journal of Sociology of Education* 32(1): 109–26.

Kim, Nak Nyeon. 2012. "Han'guk ui sodeuk bulpeongdeung, 1963–2010: Imgeum sodeauk chungsimeuro" [Income Inequality in Korea, 1963–2010: Focus on Wage Income]. *Kyeongje Baljeon Yeonku* [Economic Development Research] 18(2): 125–58.

———. 2016. "Han'guk bu ui bulpyeongdeung, 2000–2013: Sangsokse jaryoe uihan jeopkeun" [Inequality of Wealth in Korea, 2000–2013: Analysis Based on Inheritance Tax Data]. *Kyeongje Sahak* [Economic History] 40(3): 393–429.

———. 2018. "Han'guk ui sodeuk jipjungdo: Update, 1933–2016" [Income Concentration: Update, 1933–2016]. *Han'guk Kyeongje Forum* [Korea Economic Forum] 11(1): 1–32.

Kim, Nak Nyeon, and Jongil Kim. 2015. "Top Incomes in Korea, 1933–2010: Evidence from Income Tax Statistics." *Hitotsubashi Journal of Economics* 56: 1–19.
Kim, Sangjoon. 2010. "Globalisation and Individuals: The Political Economy of South Korea's Educational Expansion," *Journal of Contemporary Asia* 40(2): 309–28.
Kim, Sang Bong. 2004. *Hakbeol sahoe* [Hakbol Society]. Seoul: Hangilsa.
Kim, Se-Jik. 2014. "Kyeongje seongjang kwa kyoyuk ui kongjeong kyeongjaeng" [Economic Growth and Fair Competition]. *Gyeongje Nonjip* [Economy Journal] 53(1): 3–20.
Kim, S-H. 2006. *Ai ui miraereul dijainhaneun Gangnam eomma* [Gangnam Mother Designing the Future of Her Children]. Seoul: SangSang House Publishing.
Kim, Sun-woong. 2010. "Koreans' Education Zeal Unparalleled Globally." *The Korea Times*, July 2.
Kim, Young-Mi. 2016. "Kyecheunghwadoen jealmeum: Il kwa kajok hyeongseongeseo natananeun cheongnyeongi kihoe bulpyungdeung" [Unequal Pathways to Adulthood: Inequality in Labor Market and Family Formation Opportunities of Young Adults in Korea]. *Social Sciences Review* 27(2): 27–52.
Kim, Yu-Sun. 2015. "Han'guk nodong sijang ui jindankwa kwaje" [Diagnosis and Issues of the Korean Labor Market]. KLSI Issue Paper No. 6. Seoul: Korea Labor and Society Institute.
KLI. 2016. *2016 KLI Labor Statistics*. Korea Labor Institute. http://www.kli.re.kr.
KLSI. 2012. "Bijeongkyujik nodongja ui kyumowa hyeonsil" [The Scope and Reality of Irregular Workers]. Issue Paper 2012, Korea Labor and Society Institute, www.klsi.org.
———. 2015. "Bijeongkyujik nodongja ui kyumowa hyeonsil" [The Scope and Reality of Irregular Workers]. Issue Paper 2015. Korea Labor and Society Institute, www.klsi.org.
Koo, Hagen. 2001. *Korean Workers: The Culture and Politics of Class Formation*. Ithaca, NY: Cornell University Press.
———. 2010. "Cosmopolitanism as a Class Strategy: A New Pattern of Social Mobility in the Globalized Korea." Toyota Public Lecture, Australian National University, March 18, 2010. https:// www.youtube.com/watch?v=8G4nteMnw7U.
———. 2016. "The Global Middle Class: How Is It Made, What Does It Represent?" *Globalizations* 13(4): 440–53.
———. 2021. "Rising Inequality and Shifting Class Boundaries in South Korea in the Neoliberal Era." *Journal of Contemporary Asia* 51(1): 1–19.
KOSIS. 2017. Household Income and Expenditure—Distribution of Income Index. Korean Statistical Information Service. Seoul: KOSIS. https://kosis.kr/eng/statisticsList/statisticsListIndex.do?menuId=M_01_01&vwcd=MT_ETITLE&parmTabId=M_01_01&statId=1962009&themaId=#E_2.2.
Kotz, David. 2015. *The Rise and Fall of Neoliberal Capitalism*. Cambridge, MA: Harvard University Press.
Kwak, Sung Yeung, and Young Sun Lee. 2007. "The Distribution and Polarization of Income in Korea: A Historical Analysis, 1965–2005." *Journal of Economic Development* 32(2): 1–39.
Lamont, Michèle. 1992. *Money, Morals, and Manners: The Culture of the French and the American Upper-Middle Class*. Chicago: University of Chicago Press.
Lan, Pei-Chia. 2018. *Raising Global Families: Parenting, Immigration, and Class in Taiwan and the US*. Stanford, CA: Stanford University Press.
Lee, Chong Jae. 2005. "Korean Education Fever and Private Tutoring," *KEDI Journal of Educational Policy* 2(1): 99–107.
Lee, Hyang-a, and Dong Hun Lee. 2017. "Gangnam'iraneun sangsang ui kongdongche: Gangnam ui simsang kyumo ui kyeongkyejikgi ui nonril" [Imaginary Community

as 'Gangnam': Gangnam's Cognitive Scale and the Logic of Boundary Making]. In *Gangnam mandeulki wa Gangnam ddarahaki* [Making Gangnam, Following Gangnam], ed. Bae Kyun Park and Jin Tae Hwang, 107–56. Seoul: Dongnyuk.

Lee, Hyung. 1980. *Dangsineun Chungsancheung ipnika?* [Are You *Chungsancheung*?]. Seoul: Misang.

Lee, Woo-young. 2014. "For Korean Moms, Family Separation is Sometimes 'Necessary' Sacrifice." *The Korea Herald*, January 22. http://www.koreaherald.com/view.php?ud=20140122001005&ACE_SEARCH=1.

Lee, Yean-Ju, and Hagen Koo. 2006. "'Wild Geese Fathers' and a Globalised Family Strategy for Education in Korea." *International Review of Development and Planning* 28 (Winter): 533–53.

Lee, Yoonkyung. 2015. "Labor after Neoliberalism: The Birth of the Insecure Class in South Korea." *Globalizations* 12(2): 184–202.

Lee, Young Min. 2017. "Seoul Gangnam jiyeok ui sahoejeok kuseong kwa cheongcheseong ui cheongchi" [Social Composition and Politics of Identity in Seoul Gangnam]. In *Gangnam mandeulki wa Gangnam ddarahaki* [Making Gangnam, Following Gangnam], ed. Bae Kyun Park and Jin Tae Hwang, 59–106. Seoul: Dongnyuk.

Leicht, Kevin, and Scott Fitzgerald. 2014. *Middle Class Meltdown in America: Causes, Consequences, and Remedies*. New York: Routledge.

Lett, Denise. 1998. *In Pursuit of Status: The Making of South Korea's "New" Urban Middle Class*. Cambridge, MA: Harvard East Asian Monographs.

Li, Cheng, ed. 2010. *China's Emerging Middle Class*. Washington, DC: Brookings Institution Press.

Liechty, Mark. 2003. *Suitably Modern: Making Middle-Class Culture in a New Consumer Society*. Princeton, NJ: Princeton University Press.

López, A. Ricardo, and Barbara Weinstein. 2012. "We Shall Be All: Toward a Transnational History of the Middle Class." In *The Making of the Middle Class: Toward a Transnational History*, ed. A. Ricardo López and Barbara Weinstein, 1–25. Durham, NC: Duke University Press.

Ly, Phuong. 2005. "A Wrenching Choice." *Washington Post*, January 9. https://www.washingtonpost.com/archive/politics/2005/01/09/a-wrenching-choice/593e714f-e6a1-4467-8771-b9a2371932b5/.

Malcomson, Scott. 1998. "The Varieties of Cosmopolitan Experience." In *Cosmopolitics: Thinking and Feeling beyond the Nation*, ed. Pheng Cheah and Bruce Robbins, 233–45. Minneapolis: University of Minnesota.

Markovits, Daniel. 2019. *The Meritocracy Trap: How America's Foundational Myth Feeds Inequality, Dismantles the Middle Class, and Devours the Elite*. New York: Penguin Books.

Matthews, Julie, and Ravinder Sidhu. 2005. "Desperately Seeking the Global Subject: International Education, Citizenship and Cosmopolitanism." *Globalisation, Societies and Education* 3(1): 49–66.

Milanovic, Branko. 2016. *Global Inequality: A New Approach for the Age of Globalization*. Cambridge, MA: Harvard University Press.

Nakamura, Takayasu. 2005. "Educational System and Parental Education Fever in Contemporary Japan: Comparison with the Case of South Korea." *KEDI Journal of Educational Policy* 2(1): 35–49.

Nelson, Laura. 2000. *Measured Excess: Gender, Status, and Consumer Nationalism in South Korea*. New York: Columbia University Press.

Nussbaum, Martha. 1996. "Patriotism and Cosmopolitanism." In *For Love of Country: Debating the Limits of Patriotism*, ed. Joshua Cohen, 1–27. Boston: Beacon.

OECD. 2015. *Strengthening Social Cohesion in Korea*. Paris: Organisation for Economic Co-operation and Development.
———. 2019. *Under Pressure: The Squeezed Middle Class*. Paris: OECD Publishing.
Ong, Aihwa. 1998. "Flexible Citizenship among Chinese Cosmopolitans." In *Cosmopolitics: Thinking and Feeling beyond the Nation*, ed. Pheng Cheah and Bruce Robbin, 134–62. Minneapolis: University of Minnesota.
Onishi, Norimitsu. 2008. "For English Studies, Koreans Say Goodbye to Dad." *New York Times*, June 8. https://www.nytimes.com/2008/06/08/world/asia/08geese.html#:~:text.
Oro Gold Cosmetics. 2015. "Wellness, The New Luxury Symbol–Oro Gold Reviews." January 22. http://howtouse orogold.com//wellness-the-new-luxury-symbol-oro-gold-reviews/.
Owensby, Brian. 1999. *Intimate Ironies: Modernity and the Making of Middle-Class Lives in Brazil*. Stanford, CA: Stanford University Press.
Park, Bae Kyun. 2017. "Meorimal: 'Gangnam mandeulki' wa 'Gangnam ddarahaki' leul tonghaebon han'guk ui dosihwa" [Introduction: Korean Urbanization Looked at through "Gangnam Making" and "Gangnam Following"]. In *Gangnam mandeulki wa Gangnam ddarahaki* [Making Gangnam, Following Gangnam], ed. Bae Kyun Park and Jin Tae Hwang, 5–9. Seoul: Dongnyuk.
Park, Bae Kyun, and Jin Bum Chang. 2017. "'Gangnam mandeulki,' 'Gangnam ddarahaki' wa Han'guk ui dosi ideologi" ["Gangnam Making," "Gangnam Following" and Korea's Urban Ideology]. In *Gangnam mandeulki wa Gangnam ddarahaki* [Making Gangnam, Following Gangnam], ed. Bae Kyun Park and Jin Tae Hwang, 13–58. Seoul: Dongnyuk.
Park, Don Kyu. 2019. "Chungsancheung'i salajinda 30 nyeon jeon kukmin 75% 'nan chungsancheung' . . . olhae aen 48%ro dduk" [Chungsancheung is Disappearing 30 Years Ago 75% 'I am Chungsancheung" This Year Dropped to 48%]. *The Chosun Daily*, January 25. https://www.chosun.com/site/data/html_dir/2019/01/25/2019012501980.html.
Park, Sang-Young. 2010. "Crafting and Dismantling the Egalitarian Social Contract: The Changing State-Society Relations in Globalizing Korea." *Pacific Review* 23(5): 579–601.
Park, So Jin. 2007. "Education Manager Mothers: South Korea's Neoliberal Transformation." *Korea Journal* 47(3): 186–213.
Park, So Jin, and Nancy Abelmann. 2004. "Class and Cosmopolitan Striving: Mothers' Management of English Education in South Korea." *Anthropological Quarterly* 77(4): 645–72.
Parker, John. 2009. "Burgeoning Bourgeoisie." *The Economist*, February 12. https://www.economist.com/sites/default/files/special-reports-pdfs/13092764.pdf.
Parreñas, Rachel. 2005. *Children of Global Migration: Transnational Families and Gendered Woes*. Stanford, CA: Stanford University Press.
Pe-Pua, Rogelia, Colleen Mitchell, Stephen Castles, and Robyn Iredale. 1998. "Astronaut Families and Parachute Children: Hong Kong Immigrants in Australia." In *The Last Half-Century of Chinese Overseas*, ed. Elizabeth Shin, 279–98. Hong Kong: Hong Kong University Press.
Phelan, Hayley. 2015. "Looking Like Money: How Wellness Became the New Luxury Status Symbol." *Vogue*, January 15. https://www.vogue.com/article/health-wellness-luxury-status-symbol.
Piketty, Thomas. 2014. *Capital in the Twenty-First Century*. Cambridge, MA: Harvard University Press.

Pinches, Michael, ed. 1999. *Culture and Privilege in Capitalist Asia*. New York: Routledge.
Pressman, Steven. 2007. "The Decline of the Middle Class: An International Perspective." *Journal of Economic Issues* 41(1): 181–200.
Reeves, Richard. 2017a. *Dream Hoarders: How the American Upper Middle Class Is Leaving Everyone Else in the Dust, Why That Is a Problem, and What to Do about It*. Washington, DC: Brookings Institution.
———. 2017b. "Stop Pretending You're Not Rich." *New York Times*, June 10. https://www.nytimes.com/2017/06/10/opinion/sunday/stop-pretending-youre-not-rich.html.
Robbins, Bruce. 1998. "Actually Existing Cosmopolitanism." In *Cosmopolitics: Thinking and Feeling Beyond the Nation*, ed. Pheng Cheah and Bruce Robbins, 1–19. Minneapolis: University of Minnesota.
Robison, Richard, and David Goodman. 1996. *The New Rich in Asia: Mobile Phones, McDonald's and Middle-Class Revolution*. New York: Routledge.
Ryu, Kyung-joon. 2012. "Sodeuk yangkeukhwa haesoreul wihayeo" [For Resolving the Income Polarization]. *KDI Focus* 15: 1–8.
Savage, Mike, Niall Cunningham, Fiona Devine, Sam Friedman, Daniel Laurison, Lisa Mackenzie, Andrew Miles, Helene Snee, and Paul Wakeling. 2015. *Social Class in the 21st Century*. New York: Penguin Books.
SBS. 2007. *Gangnam eomma ddarajapki* [Catching up with Gangnam Mothers]. Television series, Seoul Broadcasting System.
Schielke, Samuli. 2012. "Living in the Future Tense: Aspiring for World and Class in Provincial Egypt." In *The Global Middle Classes: Theorizing through Ethnography*, ed. Heiman, Rachel, Carla Freeman, and Mark Liechty, 31–56. Santa Fe, NM: School for Advanced Research Press.
Schor, Juliet. 1998. *The Overspent American: Why We Want What We Don't Need*. New York: Basic Books.
Seth, Michael. 2002. *Education Fever Society, Politics, and the Pursuit of Schooling in South Korea*. Honolulu: University of Hawaii Press.
Sherman, Rachel. 2017. *Uneasy Street: The Anxieties of Affluence*. Princeton, NJ: Princeton University Press.
Shin, Gi-Wook, and Kyung-Sup Chang. 2000. "Social Crisis in Korea." In *Korea Briefing 1997–1999: Challenges and Changes at the Turn of the Century*, ed. Kongdan Oh, 75–99. Armonk, NY: M. E. Sharpe.
Shin, Hyungjung. 2014. "Social Class, Habitus, and Language Learning: The Case of Korean Early Study-Abroad Students." *Journal of Language, Identity, and Education* 13: 99–103.
Shin, Kwang-Yeong. 2012. "Economic Crisis, Neoliberal Reforms, and the Rise of Precarious Work in South Korea." *American Behavioral Scientist* 20 (December): 1–19.
———. 2013. *Han'guk sahoe bulpyeongdeung yeongu* [A Study of Korea's Inequality]. Seoul: Humanitas.
———. 2015. "Chungsancheung wigi" [Middle Class Crisis]. In *Bulpyeongdeung Han'guk, Bokji kukgareul ggumgguda* [Unequal Korea, Dreaming a Welfare Nation], ed. Jung-Woo Lee, Chang-Kon Lee, Kwang-Yeong Shin, Yun-Tae Kim, and Se-Hoon Ko, plus 23 Others 55–68. Seoul: Humanitas.
Shin, Kwang-Yeong, and Ju Kong. 2014. "Why Does Inequality in South Korea Continue to Rise." *Korean Journal of Sociology* 48(6): 31–48.
Shin Dong-A. 1996. "Han'guk'in eun nakcheonga: 10 myongjung 8 myong'i 'naneun chungsancheung isang'" [Koreans are Optimists: 8 out of 10 regard themselves as higher than Chungsancheung." January issue.

Son, Jung-Mok. 2003. *Seoul dosi kyehyek iyagi* [The Story of Seoul Urban Planning]. 5 vols. Seoul: Hanul.
Son, Nak Gu. 2008. *Budongsan kyekeup sahoe* [Real Estate Class Society]. Seoul: Humanitas.
Song, K-Y. 2008. *Jinan 20 nyeon sakyoyuk chuse* [The Trend of Private Education for the Last 20 Years]. Seoul: National Association of Professors for Democratic Society.
Steger, Manfred. 2009. *Globalization: A Very Short Introduction*. Oxford: Oxford University Press.
Steger, Manfred, and Ravi Roy. 2021. *Neoliberalism: A Very Short Introduction*. 2nd ed. Oxford: Oxford University Press.
Stelio, Nedahl. 2015. "Is Wellness the New Status Symbol?" *Sydney Morning Herald*, January 22. https://www.smh.com.au/lifestyle/health-and-wellness/is-wellness-the-new-status-symbol-20150122-12vi62.html.
Stewart, Matthew. 2018. "The Birth of the New American Aristocracy." *The Atlantic*, June 15. https://www.theatlantic.com/magazine/archive/2018/06/the-birth-of-a-new-american-aristocracy/559130/.
Stiglitz, Joseph. 2011. "Inequality: Of the 1%, by the 1%, for the 1%," *Vanity Fair*, May. https://www.vanityfair.com/news/2011/05/top-one-percent-201105.
———. 2012. *The Price of Inequality: How Today's Divided Society Endangers Our Future*. New York: W. W. Norton.
Thomas, Dana. 2008. *Deluxe: How Luxury Lost Its Luster*. New York: Penguin Books.
Tomba, Luigi. 2004. "Creating an Urban Middle Class: Social Engineering in Beijing." *China Journal* 51 (January): 1–26.
Um, In-ho. 2015. "Bulanhan Han'guk ui chungsancheung (I)" [The Anxious Korean Middle Class I]. Dongponews.net, September 3. http://www.dongponews.net/news/articleView.html?idxno=29807.
Veblen, Thorstein. 1967. *The Theory of the Leisure Class*. New York: Viking.
Wacquant, Löic J. D. 1991. "Making Class: The Middle Class(es) in Social Theory and Social Structure." In *Bringing Class Back In*, ed. Scott McNall, Rhonda Levine, and Richard. Fantasia, 39–64. New York: Westview.
Wallerstein, Immanuel. 1974. *The Modern World System*, Vol. 1. New York: Academic Press.
Wang, Jianying, and Deborah Davis. 2010. "China's New Upper Middle Classes: The Importance of Occupational Disaggregation." In *China's Emerging Middle Class*, ed. Cheng Li, 157–76. Washington, DC: Brookings Institution Press.
Waters, Johanna. 2005. "Transnational Strategies and Education in the Contemporary Chinese Diaspora." *Global Networks* 5(4): 359–77.
———. 2009. "Transnational Geographies of Academic Distinction: The Role of Social Capital in the Recognition and Evaluation of 'Overseas' Credentials." *Globalisation, Societies and Education* 7(2): 113–29.
Weenink, Don. 2007. "Cosmopolitan and Established Resources of Power in the Education Arena." *International Sociology* 22: 492–516.
———. 2008. "Cosmopolitanism as a Form of Capital: Parents Preparing Their Children for a Globalizing World." *Sociology* 42(6): 1089–106.
World Bank. 1993. *The East Asian Miracle: Economic Growth and Public Policy*. New York: Oxford University Press.
World Inequality Database. 2015. https://wid.world/.
Yang, Jonghoe. 1999. "Class Culture or Culture Class? Lifestyles and Cultural Tastes of the Korean Middle Class." In *East Asian Middle Classes in Comparative Perspective*, ed. Hsin-Huang Michael Hsiao. Taipei: Academia Sinica.

Yang, Myungji. 2012. "The Making of the Urban Middle Class in South Korea (1961–1979): Nation-Building, Discipline, and the Birth of the Ideal Nation Subjects." *Sociological Quarterly* 82(3): 424–45.
——. 2018a. *From Miracle to Mirage: The Making and Unmaking of the Korean Middle Class, 1960–2015*. Ithaca, NY: Cornell University Press.
——. 2018b. "The Rise of 'Gangnam Style': Manufacturing the Urban Middle Class in Seoul, 1976–1996." *Urban Studies* 55(15): 3404–20.
Yee, Jaeyeol. 2014. "Chungsancheungi sarajin seomin sahoe ui deungjang" [The Rise of a *Seomin* Society in the Wake of Middle Class Disappearance]. In *Dangsineun chungsancheung ipnigga?* [Are You *Chungsancheung*?], ed. W. Kang, S. Ahn, J. Yee, and I. Choi, 111–63. Seoul: 21-seki Books.
Yoon, Ja Young, J. Yoon, M. Choi, S. Kim, J. Lim, Y. Kim, Y. Yeo. 2014. *Chungsancheung hyeongseong kwa jaesaengsan* [Middle Class Formation and Reproduction]. Sejong City, Korea: Korea Labor Institute.
Zhang, Li. 2010. *In Search of Paradise: Middle Class Living in a Chinese Metropolis*. Ithaca, NY: Cornell University Press.
Zunz, Olivier. 2002. "Introduction: Social Contracts under Stress." In *Social Contracts under Stress: The Middle Classes of America, Europe, and Japan at the Turn of the Century*, ed. Olivier Zunz, Leonard Schoppa, and Nobuhiro Hiwatari, 1–17. New York: Russell Sage Foundation.
Zunz, Olivier, Leonard Schoppa, and Nobuhiro Hiwatari, eds. 2002. *Social Contracts under Stress: The Middle Classes of America, Europe, and Japan at the Turn of the Century*. New York: Russell Sage Foundation.

Index

anticommunism, 19–20
anxiety, 5, 12, 124
Apgujeongdong district, Gangnam, 72, 73, 78, 113. *See also* Gangnam
Asian financial crisis (1997), 2, 19, 26–30, 53, 81, 103, 119. *See also* global financial crisis (2007–2008)

body as status symbol, 62–65, 122
bok buin, 71
Bourdieu, Pierre, 14–15, 18, 116–17, 125–26
Brown, Phillip, 124

Canada, 86, 102, 104, 110, 115, 131n6
chaebols, 11–12, 27, 41, 42–43, 46, 130n3 (ch. 2)
Chang, Kyung-Sup, 20, 107, 108
China: consumption in, 55; economic system in, 22, 45; educational migration from, 102; education system in, 84, 112; terms for middle class in, 129n1
Cho, Hae-joang, 96
Cho, Kuk, 80, 83, 85, 97
Choi, Sun Sil, 84
Chun, Doo Hwan, 88, 95
Chungdamdong district, Gangnam, 61, 72, 74, 113. *See also* Gangnam
chungsancheung: consumption and, 53; defined, 20–21; identity of, 31–33; as the Korean middle class, 21–22; political messaging on, 22; as social contract, 23. *See also* middle class
class: Bourdieu on concept of, 14–15, 18, 116–17, 125–26; Gangnam development and, 16–17, 74–78; meritocracy and, 7–8, 10, 12; morality and, 12, 24–26, 61, 80, 114–15; reproduction of, through educational system, 98–100. *See also* inequality; middle class; upper middle class
class distinction, 4, 125–27
class privilege, 5, 6–7, 11, 80–82
Clifford, James, 115
Confucianism, 12, 56, 57, 84, 85, 106–8. *See also* morality and class
conglomerate (chaebol) firms, 11–12, 27, 41, 42–43, 46, 130n3 (ch. 2)

consumption, 26, 53–54; in China, 22; class distinction through, 4, 5, 8, 16, 121; of food, 57–59, 64; of luxury goods *(myongpoom)*, 54–56, 60, 65–66, 121–22; patterns in Korea, 11, 12–13, 16; of traditional Korean products, 56; *wellbing* culture, 57–60, 121. *See also* quality of life standards
cosmetic surgery, 63–64
cosmopolitanism, 61, 82, 114–15
COVID-19 pandemic, 121
The Cult of the Luxury Brand (Chadha and Husband), 55
cultural capital, 8, 9, 81, 97, 110, 114–17, 125, 126
Currid-Halkett, Elizabeth, 8, 9

Daechidong district, Gangnam, 81, 92, 113. *See also* Gangnam
Daewon Foreign Language High School, 90, 111
Deluxe (Thomas), 56
Dream Hoarders (Reeves), 6

early study abroad, 17, 104–6, 110. *See also* global education
economic polarization, 47–49, 120. *See also* inequality
education, 17, 123; academic achievement in, 130nn1–2 (ch. 5), 131n4; in China, 84, 112; class reproduction through system of, 98–100; costs of, 30; in English language skills, 17, 82, 102–4, 109–10; in Gangnam, 16, 71, 92–94, 98–99; graduation outcomes, 29–30; *hagwons*, 16, 88, 90–92, 94, 97, 99, 111, 113, 122; High School Equalization Policy, 69, 86–88, 123; high school stratification, 87, 88–90; *jasako* schools, 90, 95; *kyoyuk'yul* (education fever), 84–86; meritocracy in, 7–8; Middle School Equalization Policy, 87; mothers as managers of, 92–94, 114; neoliberalism and, 86, 95–98; in the Netherlands, 112–13; political scandals in, 83–84; private schools, 17, 87, 90–92, 131n6; *teukmokko*, 89, 95; uncertainty of Korean system of, 84–86, 102, 131n3; university system, 88; zoning laws and, 7. *See also* global education; wild geese families

educational migration. *See* global education
egalitarianism, 17, 84–85, 86, 87
Ehrenreich, Barbara, 8–9
embodied cultural capital, 117
English language skills, 17, 82, 102–4, 109–10. *See also* global education
European middle class, 24–26. *See also* Great Britain
Ewha Womans University, 24, 131n4

family ceremonies, 56–57
Fear of Falling (Ehrenreich), 8–9
financial crisis. *See* Asian financial crisis (1997); global financial crisis (2007–2008)
food consumption, 57–59, 64
Frank, Robert, 65

Gangnam: Apgujeongdong district, 72, 73, 78, 113; Chungdamdong district, 61, 72, 74, 113; class making in, 16–17, 74–79; culture of, 67, 72–74; Daechidong district, 81, 92, 113; development of, 67–70, 122–23, 130nn2–3 (ch. 4); education in, 16, 71, 92, 98–99; luxury consumption and, 66, 122; as model of success, 79–80; political scandals in, 80–81; speculative real estate investments in, 70–71, 75–76; standard of living and, 32–33; Youngdong district, 72
Gangnam-ization, 79
"Gangnam moms," 92–94
"Gangnam Style" (song by Psy), 67
global education, 17–18, 101–2; changing strategies for, 110–14; early study abroad, 17, 104–6, 110; English language skills through, 17, 82, 102–4, 109–10. *See also* education; wild geese families
global financial crisis (2007–2008), 48, 64, 109, 119. *See also* Asian financial crisis (1997)
globalization: defined, 4–5; English language skills and, 102–4; inequality and, 12–13, 124, 125. *See also* neoliberalism
"global middle class," defined, 13, 26, 125. *See also* middle class
Goodman, David, 22
Great Britain, 9–10, 24, 104, 124
Great British Survey (BBC), 9–10

habitus, 117, 126
hagwons (private educational institute), 16, 88, 90–92, 94, 97, 99, 111, 113, 122. *See also* education; private education
hakbol networks, 88

hallyu, 63–64
Hannerz, Ulf, 114, 116–17
happiness, 26–27, 101, 107
High School Equalization Policy (HSEP), 69, 86–88, 123. *See also* education
Hong, Doo-Seung, 24
Hong Kong, 34, 102, 110, 111
housing: admission rates and, 99–100; costs of, 30, 32; in Gangnam, 92; prevalence of apartments, 69–70; speculative real estate investments, 70–71; zoning laws and residential segregation, 4, 7, 11, 16, 89, 127. *See also* Gangnam

industrialization, 19–20, 34
inequality: concentration at the top, 43–47; economic polarization, 47–49, 120; economic *vs.* social and cultural, 3–6; neoliberal reforms and, 2–3; rising trends in, 34–37, 119; statistics on, 130n2 (ch. 2), 130n4 (ch. 4); in U.S., 6–9, 34, 119; wealth *vs.* income, 46–47. *See also* class; labor market; middle class; neoliberalism
institutionalized cultural capital, 117

Japan: consumption in, 55; education system in, 84, 131n6; middle class in, 23, 129n1; social stratification in, 129n2
jasako schools, 90, 95
job market. *See* labor market
jolbu, 12, 81, 123. *See also* upper middle class

Kim, Dae Jung, 95
Kim, Nak Nyeon, 43
Kim, Se-Jik, 98–99
Kim, Young Sam, 102
kirogi families. *See* wild geese families
Korea University, 88
K-pop. *See hallyu*
kyoyuk'yul (education fever), 84–86. *See also* education

labor aristocracy, 49
labor market: cleavages in, 37–42; English language skills and, 17, 82, 103–4, 109–10; job insecurity, 29–30; self-employment, 42–43; women in, 62–63. *See also* inequality; unemployment
Lan, Pei-Chia, 117
Liechty, Mark, 14, 62
logo-fication, 56
luxury consumption *(myongpoom)*, 54–56, 60, 65–66, 121–22. *See also* consumption

Market Kurly, 59
Markovits, Daniel, 7–8
materialistic orientation, 17, 26, 73, 92, 94, 123. *See also* consumption
meritocracy, 7–8, 10, 12, 82. *See also* class
The Meritocracy Trap (Markovits), 7
middle class, 1–3, 118–27; *chungsancheung* as, 20–23, 31–33; decline of Korean, 2, 49–52; defined, 14, 118, 124–25; financial crisis of 1997 and, 26–30; in Great Britain, 9–10; identity of, 23–26, 31–33; Park Chung Hee's policies for, 22; Park Guen-hye's policies for, 19; rise of Korean, 19–20, 85; statistics on, 5–6, 20, 23, 27, 31, 120, 130n5 (ch. 2); in U.S., 6–9. *See also* China; *chungsancheung*; class; inequality; Japan
Middle School Equalization Policy, 87
Milanovic, Branko, 48
Minjok Leadership Academy, 111, 131n5
modernity, 15, 20, 26, 129n4
Moon, Jae In, 83–84
morality and class, 12, 24–26, 61, 80, 114. *See also* class; Confucianism; religious devotion
mothers as education managers, 92–94, 114. *See also* wild geese families
myongpoom, 54–56, 60, 65–66, 121–22. *See also* consumption

nationalism: food and, 57–59; *yangban* culture and, 56–57
neoliberalism: education and, 86, 95–98; Gangnam and, 81; labor market and, 29, 37; rising inequality and, 2–3, 6, 15, 36, 42, 44, 46–53, 119, 125. *See also* globalization
"new aristocracy," 9
"new middle class," defined, 6, 20. *See also* middle class
"new rich," defined, 2–3, 5, 6, 12. *See also* inequality; neoliberalism; upper middle class
"new upper middle class," defined, 7, 12, 13. *See also* middle class; upper middle class

Occupy Wall Street movement, 48
OECD (Organisation for Economic Co-operation and Development), 1, 27
Olympic Games (Seoul, 1988), 2, 23, 53, 73, 89
Onishi, Norimitsu, 102, 106
opportunity hoarding, 6–7
opportunity trap, 124

Park, Chung Hee, 19, 22, 68, 76–77, 87
Park, Geun-hye, 19, 84, 85

physical appearance, 62–65, 122
Piketty, Thomas, 43, 46, 48
PISA (Program for International Student Assessment), 130n2 (ch. 5)
polarization, 47–49. *See also* inequality
private education, 17, 87, 90–92, 131n6. *See also* education; *hagwons* (private educational institute)
public school system, 87–88. *See also* education

quality of life standards, 32, 34. *See also* consumption

Reeves, Richard, 6, 7, 9
religious devotion, 24–25, 26, 84. *See also* morality and class
residential segregation, 4, 7, 11, 16, 89, 127. *See also* housing
retirement, 27, 29

Savage, Mike, 10
Schor, Juliet, 66
sekyehwa policy, 102–3
self-employment, 42–43. *See also* labor market
Seoul National University (SNU), 88, 98–99, 111, 130n5 (ch. 4)
Seoul Olympic Games (1988), 2, 23, 53, 73, 89
Shin, Kwang Yeong, 30
Sinsadong district, Gangnam, 72. *See also* Gangnam
SKY universities, 88, 90, 111
social inequality. *See* inequality
"specs," 96–97
speculative real estate investments, 70–71, 75–76. *See also* housing
Stewart, Matthew, 6–7, 9
study abroad, 17, 104–6, 110. *See also* global education
The Sum of Small Things (Currid-Halkett), 8

Taiwan, 34, 102, 117
teukmokko, 89, 95
traditional Korean products and traditions, 56–57

Under Pressure (report by OECD), 1
unemployment, 2, 27, 39. *See also* labor market
United States: educational migration to, 101–2, 104, 111; education system in, 131n6;

United States (*continued*)
  inequality in, 6–9, 34, 119; middle class identity in, 24–26; Occupy Wall Street movement in, 48; wellness culture in, 64–65
university education system, 88. *See also* education
upper middle class, 10–13. *See also* class; middle class

vulgar rich. *See jolbu*

Wacquant, Löic J. D., 14
wealth *vs.* income inequality, 46–47. *See also* inequality
weddings, 56–57
Weenink, Don, 112, 117

wellbing (well-being) culture, 57–60, 121. *See also* consumption
wellness trends, 57–60, 64–65. *See also* consumption
wild geese families, 17, 101–2, 106–10. *See also* global education; mothers as education managers
World Top Income Database, 43–44

Yang, Myungji, 22, 76, 78
yangban culture, 56–57, 84
Yonsei University, 88, 90
Youngdong district, Gangnam, 72. *See also* Gangnam

zoning laws, 4, 7, 11, 16, 89, 127. *See also* residential segregation

www.ingramcontent.com/pod-product-compliance
Lightning Source LLC
Chambersburg PA
CBHW031457160426
43195CB00010BB/1005